UNDER THE SKIRT

TRANSGENDER ISSUES FOR CISGENDER PEOPLE

Deborah R Ballard

Copyright © 2022 Deborah R Ballard All rights reserved

The characters and events portrayed in this book are fictitious. Any similarity to real persons, living or dead, is coincidental and not intended by the author.

No part of this book may be reproduced, or stored in a retrieval system, or transmitted in any form or by any means, electronic, mechanical, photocopying, recording, or otherwise, without express written permission of the publisher.

ISBN-13: 9798432675606

Printed in the United States of America All rights reserved.

Disclaimer

This project is based on a great deal of personal experience and research. It is an attempt to provide the result of 50+ years of research and discoveries resulting from my own gender dysphoria as a transgender woman forced to live as a man. This includes feedback from therapists, psychologists, other transgender men and women in individual discussions as well as support groups.

The author accepts the right of individuals to hold their own political, religious, and social views. There is no intention to offend anyone. If you wish to take offense, that is your choice. It is not my primary intent.

I hope this book will be helpful to those who are dealing with people who are transphobic based on their religious beliefs as conservative Christians. Many Christian sects are not transphobic or homophobic. They are very accepting of LGBT members in their churches. Some churches even have LGBT deacons, elders, and even pastors. This book includes several scriptural interpretations preached by these churches.

TABLE OF CONTENTS

Page 5 of 219

Page 6 of 219

Page 12 of 219

Page 13 of 219

1 >Introduction

In 2002, a psychologist and crossdresser named Richard Novic shocked the world when he ran the FIRST empirical study of transgender people ever conducted in the United States. The most shocking part of his carefully conducted survey was that **25% of the respondents had attempted suicide** at some point in their lives.

These findings seemed so incredible that, like good scientists, another group conducted an even more extensive and more comprehensive study and discovered that the original research WAS wrong. Over **45% percent of the respondents had attempted suicide!**

This study was so shocking that a website in the U.K. created a suicide hotline specifically for Transgender people. After nearly three years of operation and following up on as many callers as possible, even though they were talking to trained operators, **over 35% of the callers were dead within a year of making that first call**.

Only 1.4% of the total population attempts suicide, and only 4% of all teenagers attempt suicide. Most have ideation, some make plans, but very few carry out a plan that they expect will kill them. Yet 40-50% of the transgender population, **over 30 times the national average** for the United States, were attempting suicide.

Even worse, the average number of actual deaths among the general population who attempt suicide is only 10% within two years. Combining these findings suggests that **transgender teens are over 30 times more likely to end their lives** either by an apparent suicide or by staging an "accident" that is fatal. Accidental overdoses on opiates, recreational drugs, or prescription drugs. Getting drunk and driving down a curvy mountain road until they go over the cliff are often suicides staged as accidents. Some just walk in front of a large vehicle without warning.

The world was shocked when a transgender girl named Leelah Alcorn announced on several social media channels and BBS groups that she would kill herself. Fifteen minutes after her last tweets and posts, she walked down the road about a mile and stepped in front of a large truck that killed her instantly.

Even more tragic was the investigation that followed. Leelah Alcorn had been complaining for a few MONTHS that her therapist was **forcing her to be a boy**. Her parents **took her out of school,** so she couldn't talk to LGBT friends. They took her cell phone and computer. They only allowed her to use them for homeschooling. Furthermore, once the story broke, **her parents DEMANDED that police report her as male** and use Josh, her male name, in all police reports. The police **reported it as an accident instead of a suicide**.

Leelah was subjected to "Conversion Therapy" in a very mild form.

Leelah's story is not unique. There are an estimated 1.4 million to 3 million transgender people in the United States. Less than half are "out," and less than half of those have started their transition—many transgender people transition later in life, even during retirement. In a survey of all students ages 11-19, approximately 10% were 'Gender Variant.' Somewhere on the transgender spectrum.

1.1   MISINFORMATION AND J.K. ROWLING

My inspiration for writing this book was some of the statements made by J.K. Rowling about Transgender kids.

The problem isn't J.K. Rowling, a cisgender woman who has no transgender children, brothers, or sisters. As a result, she did little research and relied on the input of some well-meaning, if misguided, friends.

The average cisgender person might have seen a few hours of television programming. Programs such as "I am Cait" on TLC. This show covered the transition of the famous Olympic star and stepfather to the Kardashian sisters. As a man, Bruce Jenner became a reality T.V. star. Meanwhile, he silently and privately struggled with his own transgender identity. This struggle had been going on for over 70 years.

Others might have seen coverage of Jazz Jennings, the girl who began her transition at four years old and pretty much has always been living as a girl since then. The reality series "I am Jazz" is an in-depth look into the personal lives of Jazz Jennings and her supportive family. The show covered some of Jazz's friends, including cisgender girls and transgender kids her age. Jazz is a healthy teenage girl who struggled with some of the experiences that cisgender kids take for granted. Experiences like dating, acceptance by boys, and some emotional problems are often experienced by many teenage girls.

Even if you watched every episode of both series, the facts provided barely scratched the surface.

I wrote this book for cisgender people, especially those concerned about the transition process, whether the concerns be about privacy in public restrooms or the fears of letting children transition. It even addresses many of the religious concerns of many Christians. This book can also help address the concerns of conservatives who often spread misinformation in the name of "Religious Liberty."

2 GLOSSARY

Here are some terms that will be used in this book. Most of these terms are debated by various people, so I will define them here for the purpose of this paper.

Transgender – anyone whose gender identity does not match their natal sex. An adjective.

Trans – short for transgender originally adopted for Twitter – also an adjective.

Tranny – A vulgar and insulting term used to insult or threaten transgender people and cross-dressers.

Birth Gender or Assigned Gender – a gender role assigned based on the doctor's assessment of primary genitalia at birth.

Gender Identity, True Gender, True Self – How a person sees themself.

Gender Expression – How a person expresses their gender identity.

Cisgender – a person whose Assigned Gender, Gender Identity, and Gender Expression are all the same or consistent and matched. Rarer than one might think.

Gender Fluid – people whose Gender Expression may vary based on the situation.

Two-spirit – people whose Gender Identity includes both genders.

Gender – Roles, expectations, behaviors based on cultural and biological behaviors based on mammal behavior and historical behavior patterns by most people of each gender.

Alpha Male – Person who exhibits hypermasculine behavior. Competitive and aggressive.

Girly-girl – Person who exhibits hyperfeminine behavior. Indirect competitor.

Cross-dresser – Person who privately and temporarily adopts transgender gender expression.

Drag Queen – A performer whose costumes and makeup are hyperfeminine – usually performs for laughs and tips.

Drag King – A performer whose costumes and presentation are hypermasculine.

Gender Dysphoria – A dangerous condition where transgender identity causes discomfort, often made worse by families and peers who try to impose gender conformity.

Acute Gender Dysphoria – An often-fatal condition usually results from having transgender identity repressed or when the transgender person believes a successful transition is impossible.

Transition – a process of matching gender expression to gender identity

Successful Transition – successful match of gender expression and gender identity.

The following are some terms often used in fiction targeting transgender audiences.

Sissy – A submissive transgender woman or girl whose gender expression is male. In these stories, the boy's objections focus on fears that others will know he's a boy. He is unhappy or isolated as a boy. He quickly finds that he likes being a girl, even if he admits it reluctantly.

First-Time Feminization is a popular genre among transgender people, even if they are transitioning or have successfully transitioned. Many transgender women didn't have someone who supported them in their transition. These stories often feature a love interest, sibling, or friend who talks them into dressing like a girl. Though reluctant at first, they change and quickly discover that they enjoy being a girl.

Forced Feminization – is a more adult version of feminization. Often, these stories are popular with transgender girls who were subjected to forced masculinization as children. In most of these stories, a seemingly cisgender male with sexist attitudes is blackmailed or loses a bet and is forced to submit to feminization, then forced to take a traditionally female role such as a secretary or maid. In many of these stories, the feminized man realizes he enjoys being a girl.

Femininization and cuckolding – This is a more extreme form of feminization. The guy to be feminized the boy or guy is bound and is fitted with a male chastity device, most often a chastity device. The dominant woman is a wife or girlfriend, and after she has chastised her submissive partner, she finds men for both herself and her new sissy. Often these stories include pegging – the use of a strap-on device inserted anally and used to stimulate the prostate, sometimes known as milking.

Transgender romance is similar to other fantasies. In this case, the protagonist is feminized before falling in love, usually with the man or woman of their dreams. A transgender woman who falls in love with a man is straight, while a transgender woman who falls in love with a woman is a lesbian. Good transgender lesbian romances are very rare and harder to find.

Page 21 of 219

Feminization with BDSM is another rare genre that combines bondage, discipline, and forced feminization. This was a prevalent theme in the Adult Video industry because bondage models made more money. This is rare in recent transgender fiction, suggesting that it may be less popular than in the 80s and 90s.

Trans Men themes often have a transgender man who can beat a guy in a fight but is reluctant to reveal his transgender status to his love interest.

Here are more definitions that may apply to this paper.

https://transstudent.org/definitions/

3   60 YEARS OF RESEARCH

Just a quick note. I am not a mental health professional. I am not a psychologist, psychiatrist, MSW, or LCSW. So how do I have the arrogance to write a non-fiction book on transgender issues?

First, I have been transgender for over 60 years. When you are suffering from a disease that could take your life if you do not manage it well, you learn as much as you can about that disorder. When I had asthma, I learned as much as possible about that disease to help my doctors with my treatment. When my mother had polio, she and her parents learned everything about that condition to find the treatments that eventually allowed her to walk without braces.

I am an avid reader – My mom took me to the library when I was six years old. Almost immediately, I checked out as many books as I was allowed and came back every week or two after reading all of them. Over the next 15 years, I had read thousands of non-fiction books covering almost the entire range of human knowledge from religion and philosophy to mechanics, electronics, chemistry, biology, and even aerodynamics and nuclear physics. I read the Bible a dozen times. I also read numerous commentaries and interpretations. I learned the historical and social factors of the period which the Bible covers.

I studied human behavior – By the time I was 13, I was too intelligent for my own good but lacked social skills. I was much like Sheldon Cooper on Big Bang Theory. As a result, my parents demanded that I interact with kids my age. This activity led me to participate in numerous church youth groups, choirs, theater programs, 12-step programs, leadership training programs, and LGBT organizations.

These interactions gave me an acute and in-depth understanding of people's motivations, fears, pains, joys. They made me very empathetic and understanding of the issues of others. I sponsored dozens of people, attended thousands of 12-step meetings, supported hundreds of leadership courses, performed in cabaret and dinner theater, and directed others in theatrical efforts.

I also became a prolific and persuasive writer. I wrote for school papers, 12-step program literature, and wrote articles that changed people's minds and actions. I became one of the premier social media contributors when most people were still using typewriters and xerox machines to publish office documents.

My Social Media activity started in 1984, almost at the beginning of what we now know as the Internet. Unix administrators began using UseNet news over network connections based on the DOD network's TCP/IP protocol over high-speed modems (1200 baud) and dedicated lines.

From 1984 to date, I have written over 20,000 articles covering politics, racism, and gender issues. Helping 8,000 print publishers put their content on the Internet in a profitable way. I contributed to an online publisher's mailing list and protected the Internet and the I.T. industry from monopoly efforts. I also discussed transgender issues. I published on Usenet, BBS boards, private mailing lists, google groups, blogs, sites, Myspace, Facebook, and even Twitter. I particularly like social media because I almost always get immediate feedback. Often, dozens of people will confirm my assertions or challenge them quickly. They pushed me to do additional research, which I often provided within a day or two. They sometimes had to admit I might have been incorrect.

3.1 MY BACKGROUND

By the time I was three years old, I knew that I was a girl. My grandfather gave me buzz cuts, and dad made me wear wool pants four sizes too big and flannel shirts, but there was no question I was a girl. Nearly all my friends were girls. Every time I tried to play with boys, I got seriously hurt, sometimes almost killed.

In elementary school, I knew I could almost always expect daily beatings, aggravated assaults by a dozen boys, three times a day, sometimes more. Waiting until after school to complete written work was an excellent way to avoid the most dangerous beatings. There would be no adult supervision to stop them.

But in 1961, there was no literature or scientific information available to my parents or my doctors. I found out decades later that I had been born intersex due to DES, but that once they assigned me as male, there was no longer the option of reversing that decision.

The only information most Americans had was the story of Christine Jorgensen. The United States Marine named George. George went to Denmark for the procedures required to transform into a beautiful woman named Christine. Almost no one knew anything about the actual procedures. Most did not know that Christine was not even close to being the first to have such a procedure, just the first American to publish her story.

It's not that there was NO information available, but much of it was classified or destroyed. The Nazis burned books and research papers of doctors who performed such transition procedures. They used patients to test various extermination techniques. They sent the doctors to the concentration camps, worked to death, or were executed.

The McCarthy Witch Hunts had turned its ugly head to communists, homosexuals, and transsexuals. When the hearings were over, many doctors and medical professionals who had studied and treated transsexuals got blacklisted. Careers destroyed.

Until the 70s, finding books on transsexuals and the gender change process was almost like trying to find books on MK-Ultra, Remote Viewing, or the Manhattan Project.

4 Medical Research

On the other hand, I had severe asthma, which was worse by the beatings. After being hospitalized over 60 times, I became a research subject for Children's Asthmatic Research Institute and Hospital (CARIH). During the phase one research, I was such a good subject that they used me for phase two.

One test was to try to stress me out to see if my asthma got worse. CARIH put me with the girls' house mother, and I spent my evenings and weekends with several girls for six weeks. To their astonishment, my asthma got much better. I could even get through an entire meal without coughing or clearing my throat.

They thought it might have been an issue with my parents. They decided to try six weeks with the boys' house-mother, including weekends and evenings. After two weeks, my asthma was so bad that I spent weekends with her family, who only spoke Spanish, and by the end of 5 weeks, my asthma was so bad they had to stop that test. They realized that the girls didn't increase my stress. They lowered it. I was proof that the severity and frequency of my asthma could be controlled by controlling my emotions.

As a result, I had the rather unique and unusual experience of seeing an actual psychologist every day for two years and three times a week for another year. After six months, it took a Morse code set to be able to tap out "I am a girl" in Morse code by looking up each letter as I keyed it under his desk. When I finished, he looked under the desk and said, "I know that, but I'm not allowed to talk to you about it." Over those years, I brought it up several times, and he tried to talk me out of it each time.

4.1   SEX EDUCATION

I was about ten years old when my mom walked in on me. My brother and sister were down the block playing with their friends during the summer. I did the laundry, ironed the shirts, and started vacuuming the floor. I was wearing her skirt, blouse, boots, and wig. As soon as I realized she saw me, I ran to my room, locked the door, and changed into boy clothes. She didn't even talk to me about it.

My father decided to teach me about sex and puberty. I needed to know about anatomy, reproduction, and, most of all, the changes during puberty. Things went fine until I asked him why I was missing testicles. He explained that they were up where girls had ovaries and how they might have to do surgery when I was 12.

Dad was a bit freaked, showed me pictures from playboy, and was a bit concerned that I seemed to have no interest at all in the girls. A few days later, he showed me pictures of two girls together and kissing, both dressed pretty. It was clear that I got aroused. Dad assumed I was straight, but I imagined that I was one of the girls and the other girl was kissing me like in the picture.

By the time I was 15, everybody knew I was gay, but they didn't think I was a lesbian. I was what is now called genderqueer in presentation. I often made my clothes. Snug-fitting polyester jumpsuits Quiana shirts tailored to show off my 38-28-38 figure. Shirts with billowy sleeves tailored to fit snuggly and vests that functioned as corsets.

A gay friend explained that you are – If you are a guy and dream about being kissed and cuddled by a guy, you are gay. You are straight if you are a guy and dream about kissing and cuddling a girl. Before I knew it, I said, "I'm a LESBIAN." He got a good laugh out of it, but I knew it was true. It became a running "joke" for years.

5 Literature

5.1 General Information

My dad didn't have pornography. He had some photos of nudes, but the most risqué materials in the house were the department store catalogs from Sears, Wards, and Penney's. I loved to go through the lingerie, the dresses, and the Juniors' sections. I also liked to look at the boots and shoes. I knew what my friends, nearly all girls, were wearing, and I would imagine myself wearing the same things and being friends with those girls as a girl.

5.2 Soft Porn Magazines

When I was 14, I was on a trip to New Mexico with my only close male friend. We had been friends for 13 years, and our parents went to the same church. I found some magazines oriented toward adults on the trip but not too explicit. The magazines, Blue Book, Cosmopolitan, and others had some information about sexual adventures told by women, including flight attendants, nurses, and waitresses who described what they liked most.

One of the magazines talked about women who liked to dress their boyfriends up as girls and tease them. Another talked about how they wanted to dress their boyfriends up and tie them up. It was the first time I had ever heard of someone who wanted to have a boy who was like a girl. It was a glimmer of hope.

5.3 RESEARCH & ADULT MAGAZINES ARTICLES

I soon found several magazines that published articles based on Scientific Research of the Kinsey Institute, Masters & Johnson, and Hite. Even the rare article that was based on Harry Benjamin. Harry was a controversial researcher who had published papers on transsexuality in medical journals. Several pieces were refuted his findings, and others defended them. A scientific study from Kinsey indicated that 75% of men had cross-dressed at least once in their lives and enjoyed it. More than half had enjoyed it and did it more than once.

Over the next few years, I was able to find more adult-themed magazines. I soon found that many bondage magazines had pictures of lesbian couples and stories of women dressing cute 18-25-year-old boys as women. A few of these magazines even had columns written by transgender women.

I was also able to find several Kim Christy publications. Kim was a transgender woman who published a magazine. It had articles and pictures about the "Pageant" culture. It regularly featured women getting HRT but not yet getting the "bottom surgery."

Over time, cross-dressing and gender variance became more "mainstream" as magazines like Variations. Variations often had dozens of text articles and stories with only a few pages of pictures, usually couples. Later, crossdressing articles were put in Penthouse Letters, which covered common fantasies.

Still, well into the 80s, getting meaningful and helpful information from any of these sources was like mining for gold. Often the articles would even provide references to scientific journals but looking them up on microfilm or microfiche could take hours, if not days.

Even in Denver, Colorado, a city with one of the country's largest gay and lesbian communities, few resources supported transgender research, information, or support.

There was a transgender support group that met miles from the Gay & Lesbian Community Center on Colfax, was nearly impossible to find, and was in someone's house. They only met once a month. There was no literature or resources on where to get therapists or medical help required to meet WPATH prerequisites.

The meetings seemed to focus on trying to convince newcomers NOT to transition. There were almost no legal protections for transgender people. Those born in Colorado couldn't get identification or birth certificates changed until after the bottom surgery. After that, all records got changed, but it was necessary to live in "Stealth," keeping your previous gender a secret or risk getting fired, arrested, and worse.

5.4 MAINSTREAM T.V. AND MOVIES

In the 1960s, we had one of the first televisions on the block, and we would watch "Uncle Milty" doing his comedy routines dressed as a woman. For decades, movies and Television have ridiculed the "man dressed as a girl." The term Drag comes from a notation in a Shakespeare script where the note "DRAG" meant that a female character was an actor "DRessed As Girl."

DRAG may have been evident for some comic roles. Still, they used the same notation for Juliet and the other serious women's roles in tragedies. It's very likely that these boys in "DRAG" were castrati or eunuchs who had been castrated before puberty. From their early teens into old age, castrati routinely played women's roles in theaters and operas.

Page 31 of 219

In the 20th century, castration was discouraged, especially in the United States and even in Victorian England. From the beginning of the first movies, men dressed as ugly women became a staple of comedy and films. Milton Berle started his ugly lady drag act in vaudeville. He based his act on "Camp Drag" shows used to entertain the troops near the front lines, which featured a more masculine and muscular soldier dressed as girls. The soldier 'ladies' often camped it up even more to get even more laughs.

The "Camp Drag" continued through silent films, into early talkies, and eventually many different movies. Nazis literally killed all medical treatment and research of crossdressers or transsexuals in 1930s Germany and the McCarthy witch-hunts in the 1950s United States. Books were banned and burned, actual transsexuals locked up in institutions and lobotomized or euthanized.

Even as the Kennedy and Johnson administrations were fighting for civil rights, Hoover and local governments of both parties were arresting and convicting homosexuals and transsexuals. Just being a too feminine man could get you assaulted and detained as a homosexual even if you were attracted to women. Even in movies like "Some Like it Hot," the film tried to clarify that these were heterosexual, cisgender men. Men were only trying to dress as women because they were trying to escape mobsters. Even in Bosom Buddies, Hanks and Scolari were cisgender heterosexual men who were just looking for cheap rent. If either of them had even hinted on camera that they WANTED to be girls, Network executives would have canceled the show before the next episode.

In the early 1970s, there were attempts to create movies that touched on transsexual themes. Still, the message was not exactly a glowing endorsement. In the film, The Christine Jorgensen Story, George almost gets raped, and so does Christine. It also tries to link transsexuality to homosexuality. In Myra Breckenridge, Raquel Welch plays the transgender girl's dream of becoming. Still, she rapes a young man after strapping him to a medical table. In "Dressed to Kill," the transgender girl is a psychopathic killer killing any woman who sexually arouses Michael Caine's male character. In the crying game, the transgender girl is pre-HRT and is rejected and abused.

In the 90s, drag queen culture attempted to go mainstream. The LGBT community celebrated when Rue Paul "Crossed the Hudson" in a big media event. Rue Paul was a famous New York Drag Queen. She had done videos pageant championships and was a leader in the drag community. I remember this because I'd lived as a transgender woman in New Jersey for about five years when she made this famous crossing. The difference is that Rue Paul performed in drag shows and wanted publicity. I simply went to 12-step meetings and sought relative anonymity

The drag queen movement featured cisgender men and transgender women in glamourous gowns, too short miniskirts, and suggestive names. They told jokes and sang songs either lip-syncing or singing in their falsetto voices.

The irony is that Victor Victoria, starring Julie Andrews, played out in the drag community. Transgender drag queens took hormones, had actual breast implants, and even vocal cord surgeries.

Some NCIS episodes exploring the transgender showgirl scene in Vegas were a real breakthrough in media. The actors were post-HRT, and many were either post-op or trying to earn enough to pay for their Gender Confirmation Surgery. Unfortunately, these shows were notorious for misgendering, dead-naming, and history.

Page 33 of 219

5.5 ADULT MOVIES & VIDEO

In the late 1970s and early 80s, transsexuals began to find a niche in the adult magazine industry to adult video.

Several adult movies featured transsexual women, often guest appearances, in adult films, loops, and the emerging adult video markets. Many transgender women did this to earn the money they needed to get "bottom surgery." "Sulka's Wedding" provided scenes before and after the surgery. The results were less than impressive. Even though surgeons performed operations in the United States, the procedures for producing realistic-looking labia and sensate clitoris were still years away.

Other stars such as Shannon raised money for their bottom surgery. They raised hundreds of thousands of dollars to fund experimental surgeries. This funding eventually led to labiaplasty and vaginoplasty. They also financed experimental surgeries to create a sensate clitoris by converting the glans and related nerves into the clitoris.

5.6   THE COGIATI TEST (AND PREDECESSORS)

Several tests or quizzes assessed sexuality and gender variance over the ages, especially after the 1950s and the Kinsey Report. The most current version available to the public is the
COmbined Gender Identity And Transsexuality Inventory (COGIATI) test. The COGIATI test evolved from a combination of four other predecessors. The written version is an elementary test that can indicate whether one is transgender and how much their true gender may differ from their assigned gender. It's not a substitute for a therapist, and someone who knows they're transgender may be disappointed that their score isn't as high as they would have liked it to be. Therapists often use a more up-to-date version. Still, the therapist is looking more keenly for HOW you answer the questions, for example, your enthusiasm for an answer, your hesitations, and even your confusion. The therapist may see things in the interaction like "extra points" that wouldn't show up on a multiple-choice written test.

5.7   ONLINE – NEWSGROUPS, BBS GROUPS

One of the earliest places to have conversations about gender roles and gender identity was online. Unix operators created Usenet newsgroups to communicate frequent and common problems with early Unix operating systems. These included BSD 2.x AT&T Sys 3 and BSD 4.0 through BSD 4.2. It was a way to freely pass fixes, patches, new source code, and help with symptom-based diagnostics.

Page 35 of 219

Of course, Usenet also let you send e-mail, and users would often send e-mail to mailing lists. The problem was that passing hundreds of e-mails to hundreds of users on distribution lists tended to clog up the communications lines. So, the admins created the social net groups. There were groups like net.politics, net.flame, net.women, and net.motss (Members of the Same Sex). Discussions of gender and gender roles initially started in net.women. Then they were bumped and cross-posted to net.motss, and in 1985 were routed to a new group called net.motas (Members Of The Alternate Sex). Later these groups got the soc.x prefix to reduce the retention time.

In net.motas, many famous early movement leaders, including Victoria Prince and several others, including some trans men, were participating. There were some conflicts, though. Prince supported crossdressers but wanted her Tri-ESS group members to be heterosexual married males. They had "tea parties" in Atlanta, but discussions of transition, hormones, and surgeries were strictly forbidden. On the flip side were several transsexual members who felt snubbed by the cross-dressing organizations and were concerned that the group would also become exclusionary.

We began a thread to discuss the creation of a term that would be all-inclusive and inclusive. We wanted a word inclusive of both men and women, including crossdressers, drag queens and kings, people who wanted to transition, and people who had transitioned. They agreed to the adjective "transgender" after a short discussion.

The group coined transgender as an all-inclusive term to mean BETWEEN genders. It suggested that even the crossdresser wanted to be the opposite of their birth gender while they were dressing. Even the post-op transsexual would still lack the ability to bear children. Thus, the term transgender became as inclusive as possible. Moreover, it was used as an adjective to modify a noun. You could have transgender women, transgender men, transgender people, transgender crossdressers, or even transgender drag queens and transgender transsexuals. The goal was to prevent using the abusive term 'tranny' to discredit all gender-variant people. Transgenders and transgenderism are words that indicate ignorance of the entire transgender conversation since both presume that the root word is a noun. A transgender man or woman is a person, not a thing.

The discussions resulting from this breakthrough in naming, transformed the entire conversation. It was interesting that many of the crossdressers had initially come in insisting that they were what we now call cisgender and didn't want to transition.

Yet as they observed the conversations of transsexuals undergoing HRT and transitioning openly, crossdressers saw the possibility of their own transition. Many of these crossdressers found themselves discussing with the transsexual groups, spouses, and local support groups.

Many drag queens acknowledge that they wear high glam for lip-syncing shows. Then they live as ordinary women after the shows. Even when hanging out with gay men. They often dress in daisy duke shorts, tie front tops, and hair in high ponytails. They dress like a casually dressed woman.

In the 80s, many transgender girls were afraid that if they admitted they wanted to be girls, their gay friends would reject them. These girls formed the famous houses of the pageant scene. They promoted the houses to transgender women who were seeking transition.

Page 37 of 219

Several Bulletin Board Systems (BBS) began to feature discussion groups for transgender subscribers. Attractive to those who didn't have access to a Unix system, these BBS subscriptions were cheaper than commercial boards. CompuServe and Prodigy were expensive. The BBS boards had far more reasonable hourly or monthly rates. Eventually, the commercial boards, including CompuServe, Prodigy, and AOL, began to offer transgender support groups. For a small fee, they provided access to the Usenet newsgroups.

5.8   WEB SITES, BLOGS

As soon as the first websites started in 1994-1995, adult websites were abundant. The transgender sites quickly found markets large enough to provide a viable financial model. Transgender demand fueled VHS and magazine sales in the 70s and 80s, then fueled similar websites in the 90s and 00s. Proof that a significant percentage of men at least had fantasies of being a girl or making love to a transgender girl.

There seemed to be a growing demand for pictures of transgender girls. Web sites recycled old transsexual photos. New models could make a modest living by creating good content and even short videos viewed on hosted streaming media sites. Many significant sites began seeking out transgender models for traditional videos and videos with bondage themes and forced feminization themes.

Sites combined media with discussion groups and blogs. It became evident that many of those seeking out transsexual-themed stills and videos were also reading and writing blogs about wanting to be feminized. Many even want to be forced to be girls. After being forced to be boys their whole lives, the fantasy of having someone tell them that they HAD to be the girls they always wanted to be, became a popular theme.

5.9 BOOKS

One of the earliest internet businesses that specialized in the market created by the web was Amazon, which started its business by selling books. Initially, they made their money by selling print books published by known publishers. Amazon quickly found many excellent writers and even not so outstanding writers. They loved the ability to write about themes that might not be considered viable by a major book publisher. Frustrated readers loved to read them.

The result was that Amazon could start selling books created by authors. They would write, edit, layout, design covers, and promote their books via the web. The authors could buy a hundred copies and stage book signing events, trade shows, and other interest-specific events.

Microsoft thwarted the Linux community's efforts to get functional Linux systems into the hands of users. The Linux community created the "One Laptop Per Child" (OLPC) project to produce small laptops for under $100. These would go to younger children around the world. Children in India, Africa, South America, and Asia included. Technology was patented, and the patents were put under public license, allowing manufacturers to combine the patented OLPC technology with Linux, but not Microsoft.

Microsoft killed that market by forcing the manufacturers to install Windows because Windows COULD be installed. Thus Windows could be pirated onto these tiny laptops. The P.C. market was foundering, and companies who tried to fight Microsoft couldn't afford the lawsuits. Most were snapped up at bargain rates by manufacturers in China and Korea.

The Linux community eventually solved the problem by creating a system where Linux drivers got EMBEDDED into the processor chip ROM and drivers incompatible with Windows. The chip would have USB, Wi-Fi, and Bluetooth to lower costs but not a keyboard.

Page 39 of 219

Amazon offered to produce a low-cost version that would have a user interface much like a book called the Kindle. They could keep the design and hardware requirements so simple that they could keep the retail price below $100 and sell it for that much in the United States. It was priced low enough that Charities could buy thousands of them for these other countries. Eventually, these tablets retailed for under $50 each.

Of course, the sales shot like a rocket. In less than a year, Google had created the Android operating system with Linux-only drivers. Eventually, Google migrated Android to phones as well.

The "electronic book" created an exploding e-book market. Amazon quickly found an abundance of authors willing to write entire books on many themes. The "Transgender book market" had been too small to get traction with print publishers. Still, Amazon quickly distributed dozens of titles with transgender themes. There were fictional titles and many non-fiction titles and books based on real people.

5.10 Social Media

We usually think of social media as applications such as Myspace, Facebook, Twitter, Snapchat, Pinterest, etc. These services have common roots based on newsgroups, mailing lists, blogs, and interactive websites. The best ones make it easy to create and find large groups with similar interests. Many different interests while providing a single interface that lets you get all the stuff that interests you. They enable you to share and comment on what's important. Then others want to read what you are sharing, posting, and commenting.

Many sites, such as Facebook, now have dozens of transgender support groups and even special groups based on geography, age, transition status, and even specific aspects such as makeup, voice training, medical information (but not medical advice), and processes.

Specialty sites like crossdressers.com, Susan's Playground, and the Transgender Legal Defense and Education Fund. They provide excellent articles and forums and conduct some of the most extensive and insightful transgender surveys.

> The average cisgender man or woman rarely reads more than five or six of the articles available. Of those, half may contain misinformation exposed by the more extensive, more significant conversations.

6 OTHER BACKGROUND

6.1 12-STEP PROGRAMS

Disclaimer: I am not a spokesperson for any of these organizations. In 1977, my late father went into a treatment center. My late mom and I were required to go to some Al-anon meetings. After sharing at those meetings, they suggested that I go to some A.A. meetings.

After going to those meetings and talking about drug abuse, I got invited to some N.A. meetings. Under what was known as the "Rockefeller Laws," meetings were held in the post office because the local police had no jurisdiction. We had to stay separated by 500 feet because police could detain us on suspicion of parole violation just for leaving a meeting.

By 1980, I had quit using entirely, and after a year clean and sober and doing the 12-steps, my sponsor saw that I was a good writer and asked me to submit my story. I had to type up to 25 pages on standard watermarked paper, put it into a sealed unlabeled envelope, and hand it to him a week later.

The Basic Text came out about four years later, and my story wasn't in there. The editors took apart sentences. These were "sliced and diced" into the book's core. Some parts now get read at every meeting. They included everything I wrote somewhere in the book. Eleven years later, I would contribute to another such book on "How and Why."

Over the following 40 years, I have been to thousands of meetings, hearing people share some of the most intimate details of their lives. I have also spoken at many of these meetings, even as the featured speaker on various occasions.

I also sponsored dozens of others, helping them complete their inventories and share them. We'd get down to "causes and conditions" such that they could see the patterns in their lives. Then use the 8th and 9th steps to help break the cycles that had destroyed their lives and robbed them of even the hope of a better life.

I helped these people take others through the same 12-steps and helped them see the patterns and follow the directions. Then they could successfully take others through the steps without supervision and teach their people to take people through the steps. I would be rich if the steps were an MLM, but recovery was far more important. Millions read my writings every day as well.

In these programs, I have attended meetings nationwide and worldwide. I've participated in discussions online when physical attendance wasn't practical or safe. I loved going to a city where I lived and hearing people in meetings saying specific signature phrases my sponsor told me 40 years ago.

6.2   LEADERSHIP TRAINING PROGRAMS

I do not speak as a leader in any of these programs. Nor do I speak on behalf of any of these programs. I am a satisfied customer and enjoy sharing my personal experiences with these programs.

In 1991, I got invited to attend a Landmark Education Introduction to the Forum. Thus began 20 years of wonderful experiences as a participant, assisting with logistics and sharing my experiences.

I took the Forum and knew I wanted to take the leadership programs. About six months later, I moved to New York and assisted in Forums in Albany and New York City. I also completed the first leadership course.

When I moved to New Jersey, the New Jersey crowd wasn't comfortable with a feminine man with a guest. As a result, they were reluctant to let me take the subsequent leadership courses.

Page 43 of 219

I ended up spending the next year assisting in as many courses as I could, usually every weekend for up to 4 days at a time. When there wasn't a course in New Jersey, I assisted in New York City. I loved working logistics and became proficient at performing the "Back of the Room." The leader asked why I wasn't in the leadership program, and I had to explain that New Jersey wouldn't accept me. Still, I became excellent at listening at supporting the leader. I could work in all positions, from placing chairs to the sound console to leading the team.

In these courses, I listened as a hundred people in each class shared some of their most painful experiences, often to the point of tears. In a matter of minutes, they saw a new perspective. It changed their lives and the lives of many others.

Eventually, I was able to take the leadership course. I had some of the highest performance numbers of the class, but since the next step as a leader required that I "burn the dresses," I opted not to continue "in front of the room."

6.3   TRANSGENDER SUPPORT GROUPS

Almost as soon as I came out, I started going to transgender support groups. Some were more focused on crossdressers, others on transsexuals, and others on general LGBT meetings with discussions on relationships and transgender issues. I went to groups in Denver, New York, Philadelphia, Detroit, Chicago, and London. In addition, I found 12-step groups that focused on supporting the LGBT community.

I had told my first wife that I was a crossdresser, but I avoided the direct answer to whether I wanted to be a girl. However, aside from some 12-step sponsors, I didn't tell anyone else as part of my 4th and 5th steps. Unfortunately, none of those sponsors, male or female, had a clue how to deal with it.

Page 44 of 219

In 1988, I met a wonderful and exciting character who asked me to sponsor him. After taking him through the steps, I asked him if he could be my sponsor – knowing he could call me on my stuff right away. When I told him at the end of the 5th step that I wanted to be a girl, he smiled, "You have to do it over!".

The second time, I was ONLY allowed to write when dressed as a girl. I had to be fully dressed and ready to go out in public. I could write at home when my wife took the kids with her to her mother's house for the weekend. It was amazing how many things I had never written came pouring out. After nine years of doing the steps every year and taking 4-5 others through the steps, my inventories had become short, terse, and almost dull.

This one was radically different. There were things that I thought I had lost to blackouts that came pouring back. Memories too painful to recount as Rex came vividly to the girl who didn't have a name yet. I talked about a girl's name with my mom, but I didn't like any of those names. Ernestine? Doris? Darlene? Regina? It took a few weeks to become comfortable with Debbie. I wanted a name that wouldn't draw attention, and I had a dozen close friends named Debbie.

6.4   THE GAY LIBERATION MOVEMENT

Because I was so feminine and everyone "knew" I was gay, I quickly became part of the gay community in my high school in 1971. The Stonewall Riots were only a year old. Denver had a sizeable gay population nicknamed "Queen City." Politicians knew that Denver had one of the largest gay populations in the country, spread for 20 square miles around Cheeseman Park. They just weren't being arrested regularly, so there was less need for ugly riots.

Before the Stonewall riots, the Denver District Attorney established that consenting partners would not be prosecuted. Police arresting consenting couples would find themselves explaining invasions of privacy, especially since they had no warrants.

In high school, dozens of guys came on to me because I was so feminine (queer). Since they weren't "my type," I would offer to give their name to some guys who would be interested, with the understanding that if he hurt them, it would be OUR word against his. He WOULD be outed in an ugly way.

Nearly all matches went well, and I was just a part of the gay community as bait. I knew most of the gay guys in school. Many of us in the theater, choir, and shows would hang out together after school, waiting for rehearsals to start. We stood up for each other, and we stood up for each other city-wide as well.

Ironically, by being openly "Gay" and not trying to deny it, I helped others get the courage to come out. My friends created a safe environment where a guy could come out and be supported. On many occasions, we even helped them talk to their parents.

After high school, I was 18 years old and able to go to gay bars. I was very interested in a transgender girl but was told not to meet her because of her drug problem.

7 STATISTICS

As stated earlier, the statistics for transgender people are staggering
and shocking. The most surprising statistic, discovering that the
transgender suicide attempt rate was between 40% and 50%,
depending on the survey.

7.1 THE UGLY STATISTICS

So, here's the shocker. If there are 2 million transgender people in
the United States. If 50% are attempting suicide, and 30% of those
people end up dead before they are 25, this would suggest that
nearly 300,000 people are dying. Let's be conservative and spread
this over 20 years, about 15,000 people per year. Furthermore, we
know from other research that most of these deaths are teens
between 11 and 19 years old.

7.2 TRANSGENDER SUICIDE ATTEMPT RATE

Nationwide, only about 17,000 teens 12-19 die each year. This
statistic suggests that even using this very course set of calculations,
transgender people make up a substantial percentage of teen deaths.
Even these course numbers indicate that the transgender teen death
rates could be over 80% of all teen deaths. This includes both
suicides and accidents.

7.3 TEEN TRANSGENDER SUICIDE ATTEMPT RATES

When these staggering rates came to light, researchers conducted
further surveys on transgender teens. The discovery was even more
shocking. Over 40% of the respondents had attempted suicide
within the last year.

More concerning, among those who had successfully transitioned and living in their target gender, less than 5% had attempted suicide after their transition. Digging deeper, many of those did not get the support of a therapist during and after their transition. They didn't get coaching on living successfully in their true gender.

Further Research by the Trevor Project showed lower risks among transgender kids with supportive parents. Kids who were taking steps to transition. Supported transgender kids reported more life satisfaction (72%), higher self-esteem (64%), excellent mental health (70%), had no housing problems, suffered less depression (23%), and were less suicidal (4%), about the same as cisgender teens.

Conversely, transgender kids not supported by parents and unable to successfully transition with parental support were not so lucky. These kids were less satisfied (33%). Only 13% had high self-esteem. Only 15% had good mental health. More than half had housing problems, 75% suffered depression. And 57% had recently attempted suicide.

The situation is even worse for minorities. Black, Latino, and Native American transgender men and women have higher suicided rates AND have a substantially higher chance of being murdered.

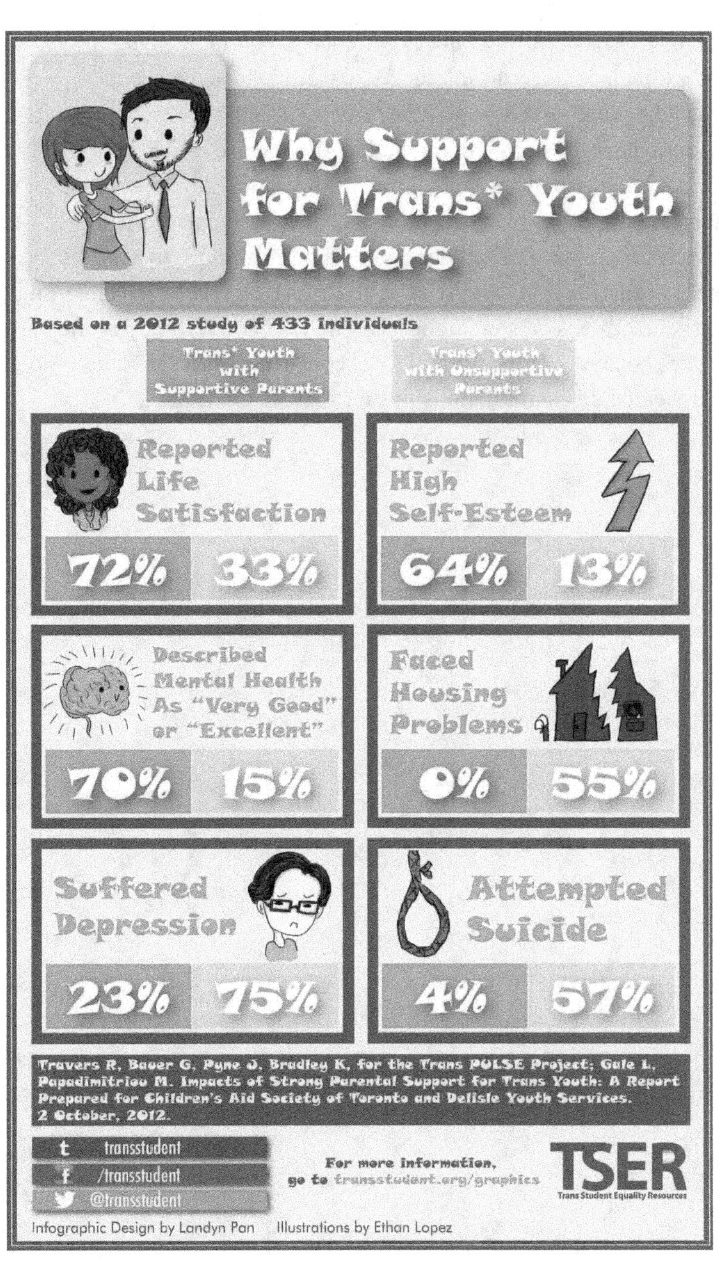

Why Support for Trans* Youth Matters
Based on a 2012 study of 433 individuals
Trans* Youth with Supportive Parents
Trans* Youth with Unsupportive Parents
Reported Life Satisfaction
72% 33%
Reported High Self-Esteem
64% 13%
Described Mental Health As "Very Good" or "Excellent"
70% 15%
Faced Housing Problems
0% 55%
Suffered Depression
23% 75%
Attempted Suicide
4% 57%
Travers R, Bauer G, Pyne J, Bradley K, for the Trans PULSE Project; Gale L, Papadimitriou M. Impacts of Strong Parental Support for Trans Youth: A Report Prepared for Children's Aid Society of Toronto and Delisle Youth Services. 2 October, 2012.
t transstudent
f /transstudent
@transstudent
For more information, go to transstudent.org/graphics
TSER
Trans Student Equality Resources
Infographic Design by Landyn Pan   Illustrations by Ethan Lopez

Moreover, this confirmed the experience many mental health professionals learned during the 1970s and 1980s. Transgender teens who were unable to successfully transition or were discouraged from transitioning had a 90% chance of committing suicide. Most patients given clinical "conversion" therapy to turn transgender men and women into cisgender men and women (modern terminology used here) got lobotomized because of the high mortality and morbidity rate. The morbidity rate for converting transgender teens is even higher than that for converting gay men. Perhaps because bisexuals could be "converted" if offered heterosexual sex and relationships on a silver platter.

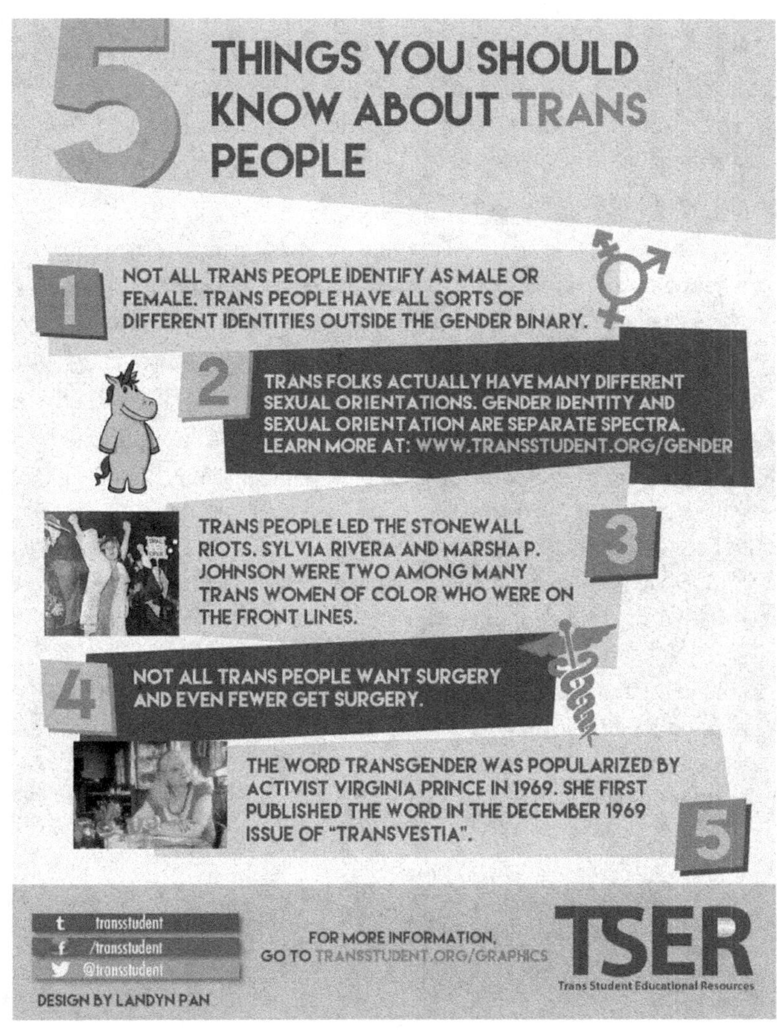

5 THINGS YOU SHOULD KNOW ABOUT TRANS PEOPLE

1 NOT ALL TRANS PEOPLE IDENTIFY AS MALE OR FEMALE. TRANS PEOPLE HAVE ALL SORTS OF DIFFERENT IDENTITIES OUTSIDE THE GENDER BINARY.

2 TRANS FOLKS ACTUALLY HAVE MANY DIFFERENT SEXUAL ORIENTATIONS. GENDER IDENTITY AND SEXUAL ORIENTATION ARE SEPARATE SPECTRA. LEARN MORE AT: WWW.TRANSSTUDENT.ORG/GENDER

3 TRANS PEOPLE LED THE STONEWALL RIOTS. SYLVIA RIVERA AND MARSHA P. JOHNSON WERE TWO AMONG MANY TRANS WOMEN OF COLOR WHO WERE ON THE FRONT LINES.

4 NOT ALL TRANS PEOPLE WANT SURGERY AND EVEN FEWER GET SURGERY.

5 THE WORD TRANSGENDER WAS POPULARIZED BY ACTIVIST VIRGINIA PRINCE IN 1969. SHE FIRST PUBLISHED THE WORD IN THE DECEMBER 1969 ISSUE OF "TRANSVESTIA".

t transstudent
f /transstudent
@transstudent

FOR MORE INFORMATION, GO TO TRANSSTUDENT.ORG/GRAPHICS

TSER
Trans Student Educational Resources

DESIGN BY LANDYN PAN

7.4   DYING YOUNG – SUICIDE OR ACCIDENT?

The biggest problem is that transgender teens are brilliant. They realize that if they admit they are suicidal or get caught attempting suicide, authorities will prevent them from doing so. They'd use intense drugs or institutions.

So, for many transgender teens who are thwarted and rejected for wanting to transition, many transgender teens will attempt suicide in ways designed to make it look like an accident. Overdoses of either recreational or prescription drugs or "accidentally" ingesting poison. Getting drunk and driving off the road, into a tree, or over the side of a mountain.

Subtle accidents are even safer. Stepping in front of traffic or pulling your bicycle out in front of a car. Doing it as if you lost your balance, to make the suicide look like an accident. Sitting on the rails of bridges over interstate highways got so common in the 90s that they installed safety fences to prevent it. Falling down the stairs, falling asleep in a hot car in July in the afternoon sun, falling asleep in a cold car with no engine running in the middle of January in a parking lot next to an abandoned building, a diner, or a bar or falling asleep on a bench in January were ways to make suicide look like an accident.

8 AWARENESS

These shocking statistics have been a wake-up call to the entire medical community. The American Psychology Association, the American Psychiatric Association and the American Medical Association have all adopted new policies. They explicitly state that when a patient credibly claims to be transgender, it is UNETHICAL to discourage them from starting the transition process or forcing them to live as cisgender.

This book is not about these statistics but is intended to look beneath the numbers. This book looks at the lives behind the numbers. We explore the experiences of many transgender men and women who have shared their experiences of different parts of their lives with me over the years. I can also share some of my own experience and research on various stages of development of transgender kids, teens, and adults.

8.1 BIOLOGICAL FACTORS

A boy is a boy, and a girl is a girl, right? Well, not exactly. This was the simplified version you learned in your 7th-grade biology class. Boys had XY chromosomes, and girls had XX chromosomes. All XY boys developed as healthy boy babies, and all XX girls developed as healthy girl babies. For a 7th grader, that was a simple enough explanation to a child who was just barely discovering the difference between boys and girls and was on the cusp of puberty.

The problem is that every element of the previous paragraph is entirely false. First, there are many different chromosome combinations. Some people have XXY chromosomes and can develop both female and male characteristics. Others have XYY chromosomes and can be boys or girls who are very masculine in nature and aggressive. On a smaller scale, genetic strings cause Androgen Insensitivity. This reduces or shuts off the body's response to the testosterone produced by the boy baby during pregnancy. As a result, the brain, skeleton, and even the body can be very feminine. In the case of complete Androgen Insensitivity, a child with XY chromosomes can appear in every way to be a girl. On the flip side, Androgen hypersensitivity can result in a baby with XX chromosomes whose brain and skeletal features are more like those of a cisgender boy. In extreme cases, the XX baby can even be born looking more like a boy physically.

There are also environmental factors. Many people remember the stories of Thalidomide, a drug given to women to prevent miscarriages. It had the unpleasant side-effect of producing babies with underdeveloped limbs, more like "flippers" than hands and arms. A much lesser-known drug, which replaced Thalidomide, was DES. DES was a compound that included a massive dose of estrogen. As a result, even ordinary boys were flooded with estrogen and developed brains and bones more like cisgender girls. On the flip side, women under severe stress often produce much more testosterone in their kidneys, and the XX babies developed male brains and bones.

I speak here of brains and bones with gender. This is not to assign rigid gender roles or promote sexism, but instead merely as a way of describing the brain characteristics found in most cisgender children of each gender. During our evolution as mammals, male mammals have developed certain genetic traits to help them compete, reproduce, hunt, and protect territory. In human development, 30,000 years of history included wars, hunting large animals, and killing predators that could quickly kill them. On the other hand, women developed in ways designed to help them bear, nurse, and raise children during the early stages of life. Women became gatherers, developing skills that helped them know which plants were safe to eat and which were dangerous. They learned to cooperate with other women to ease their burden and help harvest, gather, and process the crops.

As humans developed agriculture and domesticated livestock, they formed larger communities. They learned to herd small animals such as sheep and goats. They domesticated fowl such as chickens, ducks, and geese. At the same time, they noticed that the rams and the bulls would fight with each other. Their meat was tough. By castrating the male animals, they could pick docile male animals that would produce livestock that were easier to herd and produce more meat, wool, and/or milk. The other male livestock could be castrated and quickly follow the chosen males. When they got big enough to eat, they would be tender even when fully grown.

So, the characteristics of a "typical" male brain would be the larger hypothalamus, the enlarged limbic system, which produces more aggression, competitive behavior, and encourage rougher play. Males would have enhanced perception of motion heightened awareness of threats, prey, and predators. In bone structure, the male would have larger hands, with longer ring fingers better suited to handling weapons. The "typical" female brain would have the smaller hypothalamus and white matter, which keeps females calm while nursing. They would have enhanced perception of color, pattern recognition, and awareness of cause/effect. Their bone structure would be better suited to gathering, with a longer index finger, to pick berries and fruits efficiently even when protected by thorns and leaves.

If men of a village were killed by raiders, some of the village's women would hunt, protect, and even fight. The most muscular and most aggressive women would have real power, and the most muscular men would breed with these strongest women. Conversely, the weaker men would mate with the more vulnerable women. These men would have talents for making tools, fires, and turning poisonous plants into medicine. This ability to know and use dangerous plants gave them "magical" powers. A weak male who had been bullied by an alpha male, a small tea made from a poisonous plant could be added to the bully's soup, making him sick. The "healer" could then heal them by simply NOT feeding him the toxic plants. The first oldest profession was prostitution, the second oldest was theater, and the third was religion. Even in primates and wolf packs, we see this "theater" in omega males who imitate females, take care of the young, and make a show of being submissive to the alpha males. Yet, they can use their closeness as caregivers to get a "quickie" and reproduce on the sly.

Nearly every baby is ASSIGNED a gender seconds after they are born. If there is a penis, the doctor says BOY. If there isn't, the doctor says GIRL. Yet, at different times in the last 70 years, there were those babies that weren't so clear-cut. There were boys whose penis was so small it almost looked like it was part of a girl. Some girls had a vagina and had what looked like a penis. More often, especially after DES, there was even more ambiguity. Boys whose scrotums were not fully formed and girls with a vagina looked almost like a scrotum.

In the 1950s, anesthesia was given to the mother during the final delivery stages, partly so she wouldn't freak out if the baby wasn't completely normal. With mom out of the picture and sedated, it was most often up to the father to decide the gender of the new baby. Often, even against the doctor's recommendation, the father would insist on a boy because boys had more economic opportunities at that time. In the 1960s, the doctors would use the "phallometer." They would measure the phallus. If it was under 2 centimeters, the doctor would turn the baby into a girl. If it was longer, it would be turned into a boy. These modifications were far more common than most people knew. The drug maker who made DES was happy to pay for the assignment, but only if the child was never told of the modifications and assignment. If the child was told, the parents would be held liable for the entire cost of the assignment surgery.

There are over 300 known forms of "gender ambiguity," and until the late 1990s, these infants were assigned a gender surgically. Some estimates are that as many of 1 in 30 infants were "ambiguous" at birth. Many never knew that they had been surgically assigned. The only clue was often unusual scars in the genital area.

Page 57 of 219

8.2 EARLY CHILDHOOD

Not all transgender kids manifest their gender identity as children under 10. In some cases, they are supported in exploring traditionally boys' toys and interests such as trucks, cars, and swords, and traditionally girls' toys such as dolls, stuffed animals, and cooking utilities. Even if a child is transgender, they may have trouble expressing it. In more traditional and conservative families, a child may not feel safe expressing their true gender.

8.2.1 BEHAVIORAL FACTORS

A quick consideration here is how a cisgender child would behave. Typically, a cisgender boy will tend to be more physical. Even as a toddler, he will be competitive often as soon as they can walk. Toddler boys in daycare or groups will push each other, pushing back when they are tested. They will take each other's toys and even fight over toys, often to the point where an adult has to intervene. The cisgender girl, on the other hand, is more inclined to share, want to play with others, take turns using the toys, and even help each other out. For both groups, the behaviors are normal for cisgender kids.

So, when they were born, kids had an ASSIGNED gender, based on unreliable data. That gender assignment decided how the baby would be dressed, what toys they got, how they were handled, and how they were perceived.

In these early social situations, the toddler or young child expresses their TRUE gender. For cisgender kids, the ASSIGNED gender and the TRUE gender are the same, or at least very similar. For the transgender child, the TRUE gender is significantly different from the ASSIGNED gender. When with others of the same TRUE gender, these children fit in, are happy, and can thrive.

8.2.2 *EARLY SOCIAL FACTORS*

Cisgender boys thrive in a competitive environment and often enjoy the competition. Even if they lose, they laugh about it. The winner helps the loser feel better. These posturing sessions and fights help establish a "pecking order." This helps establish bonds over time. Cisgender girls will typically be more cooperative and quickly form networks with the other girls, doing what they could not do alone. I realize that these generalizations may seem a bit sexist, and they are. The example assumes that every boy is a fully cisgender boy, and every girl is a cisgender girl. The problem is that there are a lot of transgender boys and girls in the mix. In a class of 30, there will be at least 5 transgender kids.

Being transgender is not a "black and white" situation. Not all transgender boys will be precisely like cisgender girls, and not all transgender boys will be entirely like cisgender boys. In reality, there is a broad spectrum, 50 shades of grey if you like. Only about 15% of all children are genuinely 100% cisgender in the real world. Similarly, less than 15% are 100% transgender. So, the tomboy who likes wearing pants and track shoes and a sweatshirt may love going to the nightclub wearing a skirt, heels, and camisole with curled hair and make-up. Similarly, the "sissy" boy may wear a T-shirt and shorts to play with the girls but put on the suit and tie for church or a date.

8.2.3 PLAYING WITH BOYS – TRANS BOYS

Trans boys will naturally gravitate to the other boys. You could dress the girl in a pinafore with crinoline and tights. 10 minutes after she gets to her friends, she'll be rolling around on the grass or the mud in a wrestling match and laugh about it. She might even start it. In fact, the cuter the dress, the quicker she wants to mess it up. Put him in baggy jeans and a t-shirt with a baseball cap, and he might even stay out of the mud. A trans boy may have other friends who are girls, but many of those will also be other trans boys, and the whole group will be wrestling with each other.

8.2.4 PLAYING WITH GIRLS – TRANS GIRLS

In the same way, trans girls will immediately gravitate to other girls. Even in baggy pants and flannel shirts, she will go over to the other girls and want to play 'house'. She'll pretend to cook, wash the dishes, sing to the baby, and put the baby to bed. If asked to play the "daddy," she will put on the silly hat and overcoat. She'll get the other girls giggling at her because she so obviously is nothing like the daddy the other girls have at home. Put her in shorts and a nice shirt, and she will come home with it still clean and looking 'pretty'. She may have short hair, a boy's pants, and a boy's shirt, but she already knows she's a girl at this point in her life.

These natural gravitations continue well into kindergarten and even into 1st grade. The pattern can start as early as nursery school at church or day-care. It is so natural that it fails even if the teacher offers to let them switch sides. They will do so reluctantly and move back to their natural groups as soon as possible. Often, an observant parent will see the pattern within a few months after the child first learns to walk.

8.3 Forced Conformity

Unfortunately, there often comes the point where institutions try to impose gender conformity. The teacher insists that the transgender girl plays with boys or demands that the transgender boy plays with the girls. This often starts in first grade and will continue into seventh or eighth grade. Then it is assumed that boys are supposed to be interested in girls, and girls are supposed to be interested in boys. Observers don't know whether a boy with a girl is romance or friendship, and neither is discouraged.

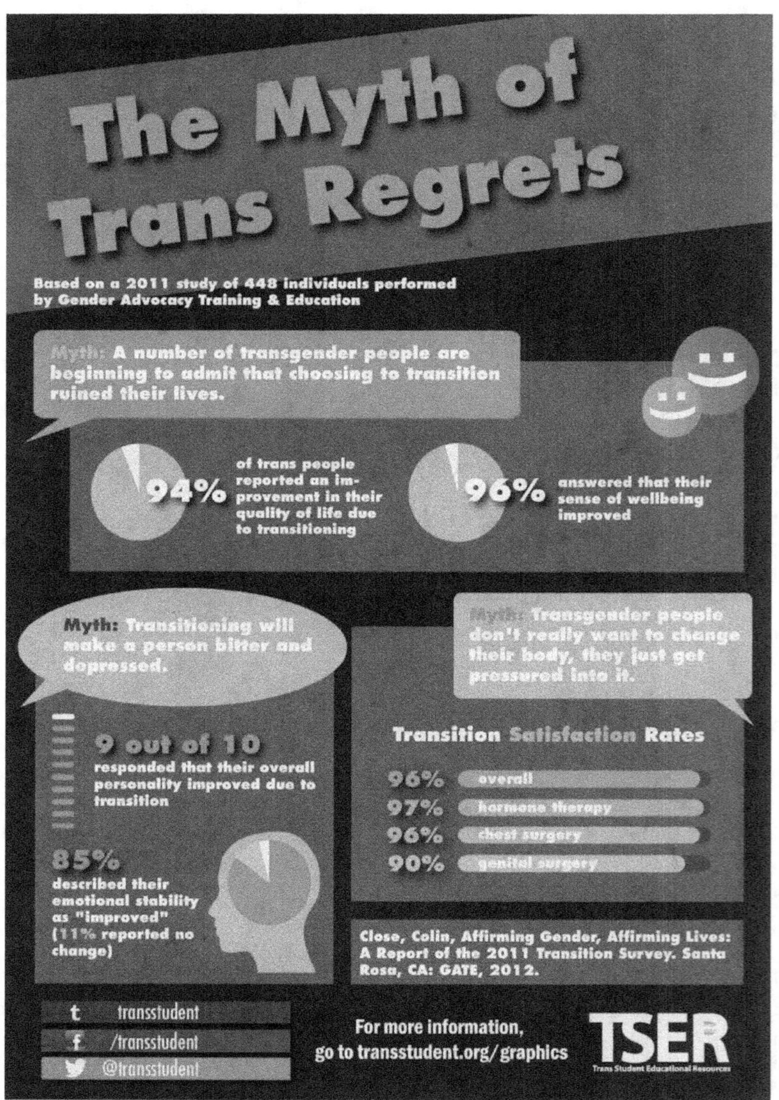

The Myth of Trans Regrets

Based on a 2011 study of 448 individuals performed by Gender Advocacy Training & Education

Myth: A number of transgender people are beginning to admit that choosing to transition ruined their lives.

94% of trans people reported an improvement in their quality of life due to transitioning

96% answered that their sense of wellbeing improved

Myth: Transitioning will make a person bitter and depressed.

Myth: Transgender people don't really want to change their body, they just get pressured into it.

9 out of 10 responded that their overall personality improved due to transition

85% described their emotional stability as "improved" (11% reported no change)

Transition Satisfaction Rates
96% overall
97% hormone therapy
96% chest surgery
90% genital surgery

Close, Colin, Affirming Gender, Affirming Lives: A Report of the 2011 Transition Survey. Santa Rosa, CA: GATE, 2012.

t transstudent
f /transstudent
@transstudent

For more information, go to transstudent.org/graphics

TSER
Trans Student Educational Resources

8.3.1 *PLAYING WITH GIRLS – TRANS BOYS*

When the trans boy is forced to play with the girls, he almost immediately becomes bossy, trying to assert his dominance and place in the pecking order. He expects someone to challenge him and compete to establish ranks. Instead, the girls don't even understand what he is trying to do. The trans boy then tries to take the toys or crayons and the paper from the girls without asking. Again, this is an invitation to a challenge and competition among the boys. The girls might let him do this a few times. The girls quickly band together and pass the crayons to keep them away from the trans boy. They stop talking to him and only speak to each other. They might even develop unique language that only they understand to further exclude

The trans boy often finds herself isolated and alone within a few weeks. Attempts to try to make her more girly by putting her in patent shoes and a Shirly Temple dress don't help. If anything, she's more likely to tear up the clothing on barb wire fences or get in a fight with boys on the way home. Worse, he may just isolate completely, avoiding talking or playing with anyone and dreading the next lonely day at school.

8.3.2 *PLAYING WITH BOYS – TRANS GIRLS*

When the trans girl is forced to play with the boys, she will try to play nice, follow the rules, and take turns, but quickly, she will be challenged, pushed to the ground, or otherwise challenged. She yields too soon since she doesn't know what they are doing. Soon ALL of the boys are trying to establish their higher rank. After being pushed, punched, kicked, threatened, and intimidated, not even understanding what she was supposed to do, she returns to class feeling completely isolated. She avoids the other boys, getting scolded every time she tries to sit next to the girls. Over time, she dreads going back to school, where she will be hurt again.

Page 63 of 219

8.3.3 BULLYING

In many transgender surveys, we see that transgender boys and girls were "bullied" in school. To the cisgender person, this might be the biggest girl in class demanding that you give her your lunch or the boy bully demanding your desert. For a transgender person, it means something very different.

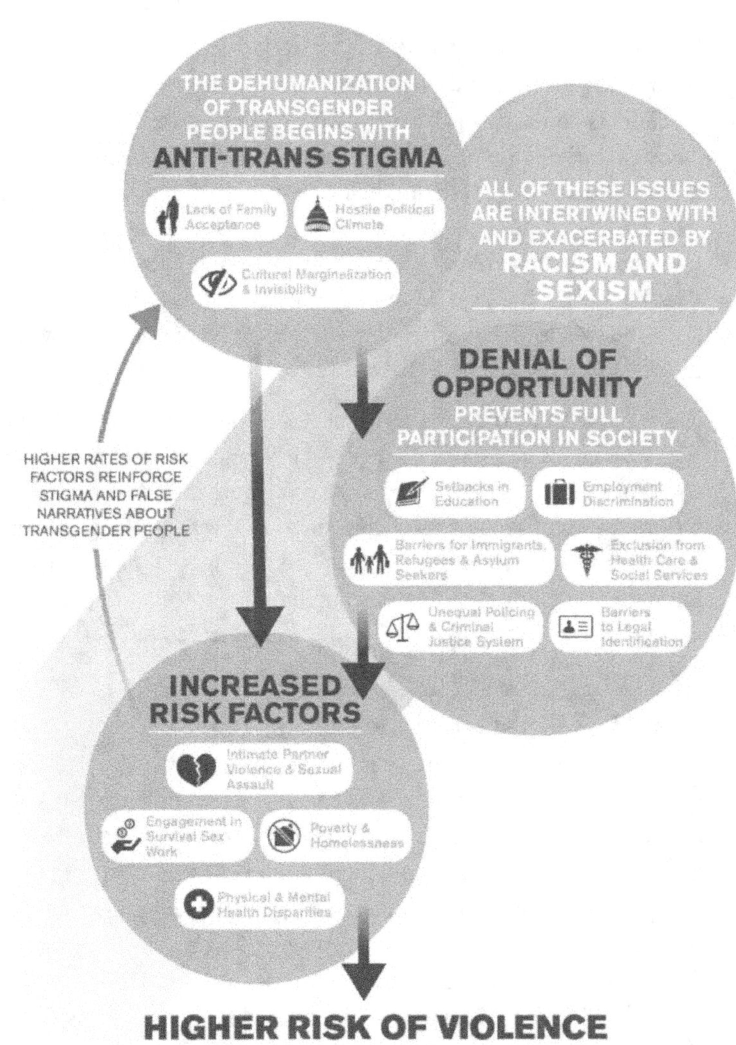
THE DEHUMANIZATION OF TRANSGENDER PEOPLE BEGINS WITH ANTI-TRANS STIGMA
Lack of Family Acceptance
Hostile Political Climate
Cultural Marginalization & Invisibility
ALL OF THESE ISSUES ARE INTERTWINED WITH AND EXACERBATED BY RACISM AND SEXISM
DENIAL OF OPPORTUNITY PREVENTS FULL PARTICIPATION IN SOCIETY
Setbacks in Education
Employment Discrimination
Barriers for Immigrants, Refugees & Asylum Seekers
Exclusion from Health Care & Social Services
Unequal Policing & Criminal Justice System
Barriers to Legal Identification
HIGHER RATES OF RISK FACTORS REINFORCE STIGMA AND FALSE NARRATIVES ABOUT TRANSGENDER PEOPLE
INCREASED RISK FACTORS
Intimate Partner Violence & Sexual Assault
Engagement in Survival Sex Work
Poverty & Homelessness
Physical & Mental Health Disparities
HIGHER RISK OF VIOLENCE

8.3.3.1 Verbal Abuse & Shunning

A common form of bullying is just verbal abuse. Making fun of someone's name, calling them names, calling a boy "sissy", or calling a girl a tomboy. Often the names and the offenses get even uglier. Slurs of race, religion, hair color or anything different is fair game. They might make fun of their wardrobe, teasing them about how they are dressed and speculating about how they should be dressed. Girls often tease a tomboy about the dress or skirt they know he was forced to wear. They tease him about how pretty she looks – knowing she hates being pretty.

The boys will tease a trans girl in the opposite direction. Calling him a "sissy", mocking him for being so girly, and telling him how he should be wearing a dress or a skirt and patent leather shoes. This is so painful because they know that she would love nothing more than being a girl, wearing pretty clothes, and having long hair. But she knows that the boys see this as something no boy should ever want to do. This is often punctuated if they are ridiculed by their fathers or uncles.

8.3.3.2 Threats and menacing

In a classroom, lunchroom, or other closely supervised environments, it's not possible to engage in any violence. Still, it's easy to make threats. It's usually the boys threatening both the trans boys and the trans girls. They might use a keyword to remind them of a previous beating or even a gesture, like punching their hand with their fist. Even a scowl, sneer, or grin can be intimidating. Often it will be a word or phrase, "after school" or "Holly Street" or "Left field." Subtle little reminders, often thrown out just as it is your turn to read, reminding you not to do too well.

8.3.3.3 Assault

Assault is a real problem. This isn't the little rabbit punch on the
way in or out of the bathroom or getting tripped. Most often, for
both the trans boy and the trans girl, it's at least two or three boys
getting them alone and taking turns punching them in the stomach,
ribs, and back. Often it will be a dozen punches in less than 30
seconds, carefully placed so that the bruises won't be seen.

Trans boys could take on one boy easily, but boys hate losing to a
girl and having the boys make fun of him. They prefer the sneak
attack as a combined unit before she has a chance to fight back and
take some of them down.

Sadly, many trans girls have fathers who want their sons to be alpha
males. Too many trans boys have mothers who want their daughters
to win beauty contests.

8.3.3.4 Aggravated Assault & Gang Violence

Perhaps the most terrifying experience for either a trans boy or a
trans girl is the gang attack. Often, a dozen boys come as a group,
usually 5 or six coming from one direction, while the rest cut off all
escape routes. There might be 20-30 punches, then getting thrown
down onto the ground, then being kicked 50-60 times. All placed in
areas covered by the clothes. Their parents have told them not to hit
the face or the hands so the bruises wouldn't be visible at school the
next day.

For many trans boys and girls, these gang-style assaults happen
before school, at gym, at lunch, and after school. For many trans
kids, getting home is like sneaking behind enemy lines. And going
to school each day is just an effort to muster the willpower to get
dressed, go to school, and face the next four beatings.

Trans kids are often ashamed of these beatings. They will lock the
door to the bathroom so their parents can't see the bruises.
Especially while taking baths or showers.

When there are more severe injuries or illnesses, a doctor will often not realize that the bruises were inflicted by many boys beating up a transgender kid. Doctors often assume that the violence was done by the parents. On one trip to the hospital, the doctor thought my parents did it.

I said, "No, the kids at school did it."

He didn't believe me and said, "What were their names?"

I listed off 12 names and said, "A couple of the boys were sick today."

One of the biggest giveaways that a child might be transgender is a high incidence of illness or injury or both. A kick to the kidney isn't always evident after a day or two. Still, it can result in too much or too little of several different hormones, including adrenalin, testosterone, and estrogen. These can alter the ability to breathe, heart rate, and ability to sleep.

Many transgender kids don't get PTSD because there is no POST. They are in Chronic Traumatic Stress (CTSD?). Like PTSD, it can make sleeping, eating, even going to public restrooms nearly impossible. Bathrooms and playgrounds are frequent sites of assaults.

Often, especially around middle school, the gym showers become an opportunity for sexual abuse. Being in the showers with 50 other boys who are grabbing, groping, spanking, and fingering a trans girl's naked body can be an incredibly harrowing experience. Especially when it happens every day. Often, Gym coaches even ENCOURAGE this type of behavior.

8.4   COVERT ABUSE

The overt abuse above could easily trigger some serious emotional problems. It could make suicide seem like an attractive option, but it worsens because of COVERT Abuse.

Page 68 of 219

8.4.1 *JUST A PHASE*

Perhaps one of the cruelest things a transgender child can hear is, "It's just a phase." This is a complete denial of who they are at their innermost core. It says, "You are not real." It says, "You are not really my child." It says, "I won't love you until you grow up and act normal."

Worse, when they DON'T grow out of it, when the phase DOESN'T pass, they become more and more ashamed that they are still transgender. As a result, they eventually reach the point where they are afraid to bring up their real feelings. It's unsafe for them to tell their parents that they are STILL transgender.

The silence doesn't mean that the "phase" has "passed," that they have "grown out of it." It means they can't trust you enough to tell you who they really are, so they just stop talking to you entirely. This is why so many parents are completely shocked when their kids commit suicide. A drug overdose or drive off the mountain. It was no longer safe to talk, and it was easier to just "end it."

8.4.2 *GASLIGHTING*

Anyone familiar with domestic abuse is familiar with the term "gaslighting." It is a slow and systematic process of sowing the seeds of doubt in someone so that they doubt themselves, making them question their own memory and identity.

When parents gaslight a transgender child, they often don't realize they are doing it. Telling your trans boy how pretty she is. How she should always smile. She needs to be pretty to be valued. Scolding her when she wants to wear her baggy t-shirt, blue jeans, and baseball cap. You tell her that you can only love her and accept her if she accepts that she is the girl you want her to be.

Telling your trans girl how handsome he looks in his suit. How smart he is and what a fine young man he is becoming. Giving him a buzz cut to force him to accept that he is a boy. Only buying him "boy toys" like guns, trucks, and athletic equipment. You're just telling him that you hate her.

The problem with gaslighting, much like the "just a phase," is a rejection of who the transgender child really is.

The dark side of gaslighting is that it makes the transgender child far more vulnerable to other manipulators. After you have forced her to give up her true gender identity, it's effortless for another manipulator to come in. A pedophile or pimp can manipulate her into prostitution, drug addiction, and crimes.

For the trans girl who is gaslighted, it is very easy for someone who finds out that she is transgender to manipulate her into prostitution, drugs, and crimes. In fact, she may become so desperate for validation and approval that she may get trapped into some of the darkest areas of prostitution, with clients who are sadists and rapists.

8.4.3 AVOIDANCE

Avoidance is a classic and almost universal theme when parents find out they have a transgender child. Each time the child tries to bring it up, the parent just says, "I can't talk about that." I've known trans girls who would go to sleep in their mom's sexiest nightgown, spaghetti straps showing, and her sexiest pair of panties. Then pretended to be asleep as her parents tucked her in, noticed the strap, even lifted the strap, and said nothing – ever.

In one case, the mother came home saw her daughter vacuuming the floor in a wig, blouse, skirt, hose, low heels, and make-up. She stared, and said nothing, walked out to the car, and walked back in after her trans daughter had gone into her room and changed into jeans and a Queen T-shirt. Neither said a word about it for months.

Page 70 of 219

The one thing that is worse than a parent doing avoidance is a therapist or psychologist doing avoidance. It might take weeks or months for a transgender child or teen to finally muster the courage to tell their therapist that they are transgender. Only to have the therapist say, "We can't talk about that." One of the most dramatic examples was a transgender girl who had just completed a nearly successful suicide attempt. When her therapist demanded to know why, she said, "I want to be a girl!" - the therapist paused 2 seconds and said, "We can't talk about that." It was practically an engraved invitation to make another suicide attempt.

8.4.4 DENIAL

Jenny, "Mommy, I'm a pretty girl."

Mom, "No, you're not!"

Sounds absurd, right? What if the name was Jimmy instead of Jenny? Nobody tells a cisgender girl, "You're too young to know you're a girl." Yet transgender kids are told they are too young to know their gender even into puberty. Children know what they are by the time they can talk.

Hearing a child in shorts with a buzz cut tell you she's a girl may sound absurd. Hearing a child with long curly hair and a cute dress tell you he's a boy would also seem strange.

The interesting thing is that if you didn't remove their clothing, a girl who had a buzz cut, jeans, and t-shirt could tell you, "I'm a boy," and you would believe him.

A boy who had long, beautiful hair and wore a cute dress could tell you he was a girl, and you would believe him.

Before puberty, gender is almost entirely a function of presentation and behavior.

Denial is probably the worst of covert abuses.

Page 71 of 219

After spending months trying to gather the courage and coming home from school after a horrible beating, the trans girl came home and bawled, "I hate being a boy. Please let me be a girl!". It had taken everything she had to make that admission in the only language she had available. But to hear her mother, without even turning away from the television, say, "You can't be a girl, so don't ask," is terrible pain.

The mother was not being hateful or abusive, and in her mind, she was just being practical. Her son could not go to school as a girl, so he would just have to accept that he was a boy. To the mother, it was just a statement of the facts.

But to the transgender girl, it was a complete invalidation of everything she was. Her identity, her feelings, her beatings, her trials, her anger, and even her love was invalidated. The topic was not raised again, even after the boy turned to drugs and alcohol.

8.5   OVERT ABUSE

Sometimes, parents and families are more overt in rejecting their transgender children. This can range from spanking a boy caught in his sister's clothes to bruising from being whipped with a belt. This kind of child abuse is horrible even for cisgender children, but for transgender children, it takes on additional dimensions.

8.5.1   PARENTAL REJECTION

The closest and earliest bonds are those of a child and their parent. The girl wraps daddy around her little finger and has a close bond to mom as a role model. The boy has affection for his mom and bonds with his father over shared interests such as sports and hobbies. When a child is transgender, these relationships are either very strained or broken. A mother with a trans boy may feel that her daughter rejects her as a mother. The father with a trans girl may feel like he has somehow failed to be a good father.

8.5.1.1 Corporal Punishment

Indeed, the most obvious form of abuse is simple corporal punishment. This could be as simple as being spanked with bare hands or whipped with a belt or razor strap. Many adults who up before the depression have told the story of "getting the switch." They had to go out and get their own switch, usually a willow branch or tree branch. The problem was that if the switch was too small, they would get twice as many strokes, and if it was too big, there were fewer strokes, but the damage, pain, and bruises could last twice as long. Of course, part of the reason the parent sent the child to get the switch was that it gave the parent time to calm down so they would not be angry when they meted out the punishment.

Part of the problem for a trans child is that corporal punishment is perceived the same as the beatings by the boys at school, only this time it's being done by someone you know, love, and trust. After a while, the trust and love just disappear. The parent just becomes another bully to be avoided. Often, by the time puberty sets in, all trust is gone. There is no safety to discuss drinking, smoking, sex, or drugs with a parent, the parent is just another bully.

Punishment, even corporal punishment, is usually based on the fundamental principle of the child knowing that they did something wrong. Understanding why it was wrong. Knowing that they are being punished for specific actions. There is an apparent cause/effect relationship.

Punishing a transgender child for being transgender and acting like an ordinary girl or boy is brutality. The cause/effect is lost. The trans child is being punished for being who they are. They are being punished for expressing themselves authentically in ways that would be accepted if they were cisgender.

8.5.1.2 Physical Abuse

Physical abuse has no cause/effect. Often, physical abuse is coupled with intoxication. Mom gets drunk and starts beating her daughter because she is dressed like a boy and mom is mad at the father. Dad comes home drunk after a day of hard labor and being criticized by the boss who doesn't want to pay, then comes home and beats his son for being such a "sissy", such a "wimp".

Physical abuse can become quite extreme because of intoxication, especially alcohol. Broken bones, hospitalization, and life-threatening situations are too common, the worst kind of trauma, even for cisgender kids. There is no reason for the beating. Only an angry parent who is lashing out at a child. Because they can't lash out at the people who are really causing their anger. Because they can't accept the pain. The pain they have caused themselves.

For a transgender child, the abuse is magnified. When doctors or teachers try to reach out to them to help, the transgender child is so ashamed and guilt-ridden that they refuse to talk about the physical abuse. They can't talk about their parent's hatred for their "sissy" or "tomboy".

Sadly, the result is often a run-away child who has poorly planned. She runs out of the house with little or no preparation, no money, no savings, and no real plan for how to survive. The transgender child is only focused on trying to escape the violence. In the worst-case scenario, the split is a result of the discovery. A typical scenario of the father finding his "son" dressed like a girl and a fight resulting in a lock-out with the trans girl wearing only the dress on her back and maybe a coat. This would be a dangerous situation for a cisgender girl, even more so for a transgender girl.

8.5.1.3 Sexual Abuse

Trans kids are often victims of sexual abuse. The trans girl is an easily identified target for predators who can manipulate them. In a terrifying combination, they can use affirmation, guilt, and shame to get what they want from their victim, then keep them quiet. The trans girl is often more likely to be "broken". They are raped and shamed to "prove that you are just a helpless girl."

Even as they become teens and adults, trans kids are more likely to be raped, often violently. They aren't even people in the eyes of their predators. This may be one of the reasons why sexual predators like to paint trans kids as sexual predators. Not only is it an easy way to keep their victims quiet, but it also shifts the focus away from the actual predators. This type of abuse is widespread where the predator is in a position of trust and authority. The athletic coach offers favorable treatment in exchange for compliance. The youth pastor provides the possibility of acceptance and belonging to the youth group in exchange for submission. The teacher offers a good grade in exchange for acceptance and silence.

At the same time, their position of trust enables them to smear their victims when they stop being compliant. The predator knows the transgender girl's secret or the trans boy's secret. Rather than threatening to kill the pets or the parents, they only have to threaten to expose the secret. If there is still resistance, the predator can easily paint their victim as a liar who makes up stories. Then pull out the trump card of telling others that the victim is transgender.

Because of this kind of sexual abuse, many transgender kids become asexual. As trans kids who have already been bullied and want to avoid the vulnerabilities of another sexual predator, they shut off their sexual desires completely. History is filled with many great innovators who were asexual. Many of them were notable for NOT being alpha males or girly girls.

Some do not become asexual. Victims of sexual predators often separate feelings of love from sexual pleasure. Often, emotional attachments make sexual arousal difficult, and sexual attraction makes emotional bonding difficult.

Victims of sexual abuse can often develop serious mental health issues, including multiple personality disorder, depression, or schizophrenia.

8.5.1.4 Emotional Abuse

Emotional abuse is also widespread. For a trans child, having one or both parents refuse to accept them can be painful. It can mean getting no affirmation, being insulted or ridiculed, and being unable to please them.

Often, the parents don't even know they are inflicting emotional abuse. A simple phrase like "that damn faggot" or a joke about a "queer" tells the transgender child that there is no safety with their parents. Parents who laugh at Uncle Dave's flag jokes or nod at grandpa's religious rants against homosexuals can clearly signal that family is not a safe place.

8.5.2 *FORCED ACTIVITIES*

Another common strategy used by parents to try to force their kids to be cisgender is forced activities. Often, the parent will spend months talking up a particular activity. Sending a blatant message that the child MUST participate. It's so important to the parent that their love may depend upon it.

8.5.2.1 Man Up – Contact Sports

An alpha male father often tries to get his trans girl "son" to "Man Up" by putting them in contact sports like football, boxing, or baseball. The child has no interest, motivation, or passion for the activity. His performance is, at best mediocre. The rest of the team often blames the "sissy" for games lost. Far too often, it just becomes another opportunity and motivation for more beatings. Similar to those they already experience at school.

8.5.2.2 Get Pretty – Pageants

To get a trans boy to "Be pretty", mothers often try to force their "daughters" into activities intended to make them feminine. Beauty pageants, ballet lessons, church groups. Situations where she will HAVE to wear a dress, where she will HAVE to make herself look pretty, and where she will have to act like a girl to be accepted by the other people involved.

Even though she is not transgender, Karen Morris provides some excellent insight into the pressures in her book "Fatlash". It describes the ugly side of forced femininity and the weight problems she experienced. Karen became a radio host, writer, and brilliant woman but never even tried to become the "girly-girl" her mother had forced her to be. One can only imagine how much worse it would be for a transgender boy who has even less desire to be "girly".

8.5.2.3 Egg-Head – Isolation & Hobbies

Often, a compromise is reached for a transgender child to isolate. Rather than force them into activities they hate or allow them to do activities the parents hate, the transgender kid will just isolate. Often parents will unwittingly support this isolation. The child wants to go to the library and get as many books as possible. The trans girl has no interest in books about boys. The trans boy has no interest in books about girls. The parents won't let them have books about the opposite sex, so they go to the non-fiction section.

The parents won't give their transgender daughter a Barbie doll for Christmas, and the child rejects the baseball mitt, so they get her a chemistry set. Instead of giving the transgender son a BB gun, their parents give him a microscope or telescope. These are "gender-neutral" toys that can be accepted by transgender children and prepare them for a profession in technology. The transgender boy may become a doctor, the transgender girl may become an engineer.

Often, this is the "booby prize", the one you get but didn't really want. For Christmas, the trans girl wanted the Barbie Doll and the Disney Princess dress, skirts, and leggings. Instead, she got the Chemistry set, a hoodie, and baggy blue jeans. The trans boy wanted the BB gun, baseball glove, hoodie, and oversized baggy jeans. Instead, he got the Microscope, leggings, and a pink dress with puffy sleeves.

9 UNDERCOVER

9.1 UNDERCOVER TACTICS

Often, trans kids survive abuse by exhibiting the desired behaviors. They pretend to be the people they are supposed to be, even though they know that it's all a lie. Transgender kids are often brilliant, with an average IQ of over 160. This is because they have to literally learn to be the gender they aren't after being their true gender. A left-handed transgender girl often has an IQ over 180 because she has to blend like a chameleon, learn in 3 different ways, become invisible and entertain herself. A left-handed transgender boy will have less need to hide her male persona entirely as she gets older. She can wear pants moderate her behavior to seem like a cisgender girl, like a chameleon.

It's important to note that even though transgender children become adept at looking and acting like cisgender children, this does not mean they have "grown out of it". It just means that they have become masters of deception. They don't trust others because it's not safe, and they know how to keep secrets so well that they can even tell the truth and make it sound like a lie.

9.1.1 OBSERVATION

Remember that earlier, when the child first entered day-care, pre-school, or kindergarten, the transgender kids naturally gravitated toward those of their true gender. A transgender girl would gravitate to the girls, and a transgender boy would gravitate to the boys. They naturally fit in, and there was no effort involved. However, suppose a transgender child feels FORCED to conform to the other gender. In that case, they develop keen powers of observation.

Remember, to a transgender girl, being a boy is entirely unnatural. They must observe everything the boys do carefully, noticing each quirk or trait. It's a bit like studying animals in a cage or Jane Goodall observing chimps in the wild. Nothing is natural, and the observer may make completely incorrect assumptions about why a particular behavior occurs, but the observations are correct. Their observations are so keen and acute that they make Sherlock Holmes seem more like Lestrade.

9.1.2 IMITATION

The next step for the transgender child is to imitate what they have observed. Often the results are awkward and absurd. A transgender boy trying to act like a girl often first appears much like a cisgender boy trying to act like a girl. And the transgender girl trying to act like a boy is a bit like a scene from La Cage au Folles. The problem is that the stakes are MUCH higher. Failure to imitate the target gender quickly and effectively can result in violence and worse.

9.1.3 ASSIMILATION

"We are the Borg. Prepare to be assimilated."

Yes, this is almost precisely what assimilation feels like to a transgender child. They eventually reach the point where they can "fit in". Well, enough to avoid the most extreme forms of violence. They may even have one or two friends of the same ASSIGNED gender. Usually, there are significantly few such friends, just enough to create the appearance of being "normal".

Assimilation is a bit like being a spy or an undercover cop. They know they can't break cover because the bad guys will kill them if they do. For a trans kid, the consequences are even worse. Blowing the cover could mean going right back to the thrice-daily gang-bang-style assaults, with even less chance of long-term survival. For trans boys, there is the risk of gang rape.

9.1.4 ISOLATION

Since assimilation is stressful and challenging to sustain for long periods, transgender kids will also become more isolated. They will often spend hours alone at home, reading, doing hobbies, and even engaging in "pressure valves" to ease the dysphoria, the pain of being forced to assimilate. These activities may include a trans boy who practices boxing, shadow boxing, or even practicing martial arts like karate, jujitsu, or Kung foo. For the trans girl, the pressure valve activities might include crossdressing, cooking, cleaning, and singing.

These "pressure valves" can often provide short periods of calm, a sense of integrity, and a few moments of authenticity and self-honesty. Usually, these pressure valves are done very privately and only while alone. Still, some activities like chores may actually be welcomed. The trans girl who wants to cook, clean the house, and do the laundry may be teased, but "his" help is welcomed. The trans boy who wants to mow the lawn, trim the hedges, and take out the trash might even earn praise for helping.

9.1.5 INVISIBILITY

Even if they can assimilate, the other strategy often used is to become "invisible". It's said that the ninjas were invisible, and Americans assumed this meant dressing Ninjas in all black coveralls. Transgender kids know how to be truly invisible. Much like the Sherlock Holmes story where the "invisible man" turns out to be a taxi driver, trans kids learn to avoid drawing attention to themselves. They know to divert attention to others and, even more important, get others to ADMIRE someone else. In this way, transgender kids can build alliances with solid leaders and get things done by working in the background rather than drawing attention to themselves.

Page 81 of 219

This invisibility can also extend to writing under pseudonyms, submitting recommendations anonymously, and even passing them in unmarked envelopes. I've known trans kids who would specifically ask their teacher NOT to praise them in the classroom for getting the highest test scores. Many trans kids will deliberately miss a few questions to keep their scores from drawing too much attention. They won't participate in class, but they will write 5 pages of remarks and turn them into the teacher at the end of the day. Often, they will challenge assertions made by the teacher, offer sources to refute them, and offer alternative interpretations or perspectives. In the end, they will ask them to only discuss it AFTER class. In some cases, the teacher will ask these students to write up their missives the night BEFORE the lecture. The teacher discretely includes these unique perspectives into the classroom discussions.

Even the clothing is designed to draw as little attention as possible, dark colors, loose fit, everything cheap, and nothing to stand out. At most, there might be some quiet comments on the lack of brands, but the interest and comments last only a second, making the transgender child easy to forget.

There are times when the school is somewhat shocked to discover that this "invisible person" is the valedictorian of their school.

10 PUBERTY

We know that teen suicides are much higher during puberty, especially for ages 12 to 19. We also know that accidental deaths are unusually high. For a transgender child, puberty is a perilous time. The general theme is the same for transgender boys and transgender girls. There are unique challenges for each gender. Especially when forced to suffer through the puberty of their ASSIGNED Gender. The wrong puberty.

10.1 ROMANTIC AND SEXUAL ATTRACTION

Puberty is further complicated by romantic and sexual attractions. Attractions are pretty much set in stone by the time a child is 5 or 6, about 2-3 years after gender identity is expressed. In fact, romantic and sexual preference may be established even earlier or partly a brain structure function. Still, the point is that by the time they are expressed verbally or emotionally, they are pretty much set in stone. Sleeping Beauty is kissed by the beautiful Princess, or the Frog Prince gets kissed by a handsome prince. Belle kisses the beast, who turns into a beautiful princess in my version of Beauty and the Beast.

Bisexuals are often attracted to both genders but develop a preference for one gender or the other. They are looking for the "best of both", whatever that may be for that individual. It might be a more masculine woman or a more feminine man.

Some trans teens avoid relationships altogether. Others find themselves attracted to members of the sex opposite of their gender identity. They are often perceived as gay or lesbian. A transgender girl attracted to boys will appear to be gay and will attract gay suitors. A trans boy attracted to girls will often appear to be a "butch" lesbian, and lesbians will come out to them. Both are actually straight. They are attracted to the opposite of their gender.

Things get more interesting for the trans girl attracted to girls or the trans boy attracted to boys. A common phrase is "do you want to date her or BE her?" Conversely, "Do you want to date him or BE him?" For the transgender homosexual, the answer is, "Both!"

This can make romantic attraction very confusing. Are you attracted to a woman because she is someone you admire? Because you want to look the same? Or is she someone you feel attracted to romantically? Often, the lines are so blurry that it's almost impossible to tell where the attraction lies.

There may be deep friendships that become romances, there may be romantic interests that can never be more than friendships. There may be ambiguity, a dance between friendship and intimacy. These can be frustrating times for a homosexual transgender teen in puberty.

10.2 TRANS BOY PUBERTY

A transgender boy wants to become a transgender man. Being forced to go through the puberty of a girl into a woman is a nightmare. While cisgender girls can't wait for breasts, curves, make-up, and being able to dress up and go on dates with boys, it's a very different experience for a transgender boy. To the transgender boy, breasts, periods, and formal dresses are the LAST thing they want to experience.

10.2.1 AWARENESS OF PUBERTY

Before 7th grade, about 10 or 11 years old, the trans boy is not significantly different from a cis boy. They might both have short hair, but their body shapes are similar, and both pretty much look and act the same. With minimal effort, a. tomboy can put on her cap and play on a softball team with the boys, and you wouldn't know that she's a girl just by looking at her. The difference is only about 1 cubic inch.

But even as early as 10 years old, girls in her class begin to form breasts and start wearing training bras. They start other less visible changes, including Aunt Flo's dreaded "monthly visit". With any luck, the transgender girl is not among the first to experience such a transition, but she knows that it's coming.

Usually, in 6th or 7th grade, the school teaches a semester or part of a semester on basic biology to explain genitalia and, most importantly, the changes during puberty. The girls and boys are separated into different classes. Girls learn about breasts, periods, and feminine hygiene products such as pads and tampons. These are already sensitive topics for adult women. There is a reluctance to have this lecture in front of boys. Boys learn about hairy bodies, voice changes, and beards.

10.2.2 FEAR OF PUBERTY

For the transgender boy, knowing that they will be growing breasts, having periods is scary. Losing upper body strength, getting fatter in the butt, and not fitting into boys' clothes anymore – is a terrifying thought and becomes the stuff of nightmares. The trauma is made worse because they have few close relationships with other girls. Remember that they have been shunned, shamed, excluded, and mocked by those girls.

10.2.3 EARLY SIGNS OF PUBERTY

Those early signs of puberty for a girl, the weight distribution, the mood swings, and the early symptoms of estrogen production often don't occur as "I'm becoming a woman." To a transgender boy, there is hyper-awareness and dread. Perhaps the most dreaded signal is "budding".

10.2.4 BREAST FORMATION

From the earliest budding and sensitivity, even the first indications
that a trans boy is growing breasts is a terrifying experience. To deal
with the sensitivity, the trans boy will try to avoid the usual options
of a camisole or training bra. They often opt for a smaller T-shirt
over a baggy one, very baggy T-shirts, or even band-aids or gauze to
protect and prevent sensitive chafing.

10.2.5 BINDING & HIDING

As soon as the breasts start to form, many transgender boys will try
to stop the growth or hide their breasts. Ace bandages, cloth wraps,
even duct tape are just some of the methods a teen trans boy will try
to prevent or suppress the growth of breasts. Later, they will learn
about compression shirts and binders that look like training bras but
compress the breasts. They often put the binder and top on in a
bathroom stall to avoid showing them in the locker room.

There is a significant problem if the breasts grow too large. Binding
and hiding a-cup or b-cup breasts is possible if not entirely
comfortable. Binding and hiding C or D-cup breasts can be
extremely painful and dangerous. Compression can become so
severe that it cuts blood flow to the breasts. For some trans boys, the
damage becomes so acute that they form cysts and fibroids. When
the doctor tells them they are at risk of getting breast cancer, it's not
precisely motivation to stop. An insurance company provided
mastectomy is an answer to the prayers of a teen transgender boy.
The problem is that cutting off circulation and persistent bruises can
result in gangrene. This is a rare but real risk.

10.2.6 PACKING

If a trans boy can pass as a boy, there is often a desire to "pack" and
even have STP (Stand To Pee) devices, which allow them to use
urinals. Many trans boys can pass as boys when away from home on
weekends and evenings. He may live the double life of being a
"girl" at school.

10.2.7 LESBIAN COMMUNITY

Often, trans boys are seen as lesbians. Sexual preference and sexual identity are not directly related. However, even if there isn't sexual attraction to women, many trans boys find support and friendship in the lesbian community. Because they have not been able to transition, they see the lesbian community as a place where they can be as masculine as possible and still be accepted. In addition, lesbians often come out to trans boys because there is the lowest risk of rejection. Even if the trans boy is sexually attracted to boys/men, he can often welcome the newly outed lesbian. He can introduce her to others in the lesbian community in their school and community.

10.2.8 NON-BINARY OPTIONS

One of the key advantages of being active in the LGBT community is to explore their gender identity in safe and accepted ways. When the transition is not an option due to hostile parents and a hostile school environment, the trans boy can be a lesbian.

10.2.8.1 Butch

Within the gay and lesbian community, there is a wide range of acceptable and even popular gender roles. In the lesbian community, women who are "butch" are often a usual faction. Butch lesbians often dress very masculinely, have short hair, even buzz cuts. They can dress in male attire ranging from "cowboy" to "truck driver" to "construction worker" or even "biker". Many of these women even work out and develop strong muscles. They can easily defend their honey from any man who thinks he can make a move and accost the butch girl's girlfriends or even her friends.

At the same time, they often DON'T bother with binding and trying to hide their breasts. When at a lesbian bar, they want the other women to know that they are women. Since sexual preference has nothing to do with gender identity, it's not unusual to see two butch women who are together, or a butch woman and a more feminine woman.

Page 87 of 219

10.2.8.2 Fluid

Another option within the lesbian community is being gender fluid.
A trans boy can be the feminine girl everyone expects her to be.
Then she can present as butch on the weekends and evenings when
she wants to go to a friendly place for lesbians. The other thing I
have seen is trans girls who would dress more masculine during the
day and at school or work, then go out in a short skirt and tight, low-
cut blouse. Their reason was because they heard their guy friends
bragging about how many girls they had bedded. They decided to
collect their own "notches" by seducing as many guys as possible. I
haven't heard this story often, but enough to see it as a significant
variation of gender-fluid women. This may merit more research in
the future.

10.2.8.3 Queer

For trans boys, being Queer or genderqueer is a "toe in the water"
approach. Rather than going to school on a Monday morning as full-
on butch and trying to present 100% boy, the genderqueer process is
like gradually lowering yourself into the water a little bit at a time.
Switching from girls' jeans to boys' jeans, switching from girl's V-
neck T-shirts to boy's u-neck T-shirts. Getting some boy's dress
shirts. It's like boiling the frog in reverse. The genderqueer trans
boy is gradually creating acceptance as she transitions.

To moderate the harassment, they may continue with the things they
like about being a girl. Hiding acne with make-up, earrings,
plucking eyebrows. Instead of getting men's shoes, they will find
black lace-up trainers or even oxfords that still fit narrower feet.
Many trans-boys have the same difficulty walking in men's shoes
with the extended toes that trans-girls have when they first wear
heels.

With the non-binary options, the trans boy will often find a "comfortable place" that allows them to feel moderately comfortable in their own skin. It reduces Gender Dysphoria enough to get past puberty to become adults. Some will drift within these comfort zones, adjust over time, and be comfortable there for years.

For other trans boys, the non-binary option is still only a pressure valve. They can get enough relief to make it through puberty alive. However, the Gender Dysphoria is still there, sometimes becoming intense. To them, the non-binary options are a way to stay in the family home, reduce bullying, and get through school.

10.2.8.4 Social Structures

A covert version of the non-binary option is socialization-based. In this situation, a trans-boy will find ways to hang out with the guys and become one of the guys. This may mean wearing girls' jeans and a bra and team shirt. Still, she is there hanging out with the guys, watching the football games, cheering the teams, drinking beer, eating chips, and in every sense becoming "one of the boys". This type of social transition without a radical change in presentation is most common with trans boys who are sexually attracted to men. When they are hanging out with the boys, some boys they want to BE like, others they want to DO, and some who are BOTH.

The tragedy is that parents, social workers, therapists, and others often assume that the trans boy has "grown out" of the "phase" and is no longer transgender. Nothing could be further from the truth. Unfortunately, too often, the underlying Gender Dysphoria is still pervasive, and the time bomb is still ticking. They are often misdiagnosed with other mental health disorders such as depression, anxiety, and bipolar. They have given up trying to talk about their Gender Dysphoria and the dire consequences that follow when they do.

10.2.9 BINARY EXPLORATIONS

For transgender boys, the dysphoria may become severe, and even without blockers and hormones, they will try to become more noticeable and overtly masculine. These are more binary explorations and are often preliminary steps to actual transition.

10.2.9.1 Hyper-Butch

Unlike the butch girl in the lesbian community, the hyper-butch trans-boy looks, acts, and thinks as much like an alpha male as they possibly can. They work out and build up male masculine muscles. They drink beer and whiskey. They get into fights they should lose yet win. They are competitive whether playing poker or arm wrestling. They don't suffer insults. They often like to gamble and make bets on their own abilities. Usually, by the time they have reached this stage, they have learned martial arts, fighting dirty, and even shooting pistols and rifles. Many trans boys even consider ROTC, military service in the Marines, and love going hunting and fishing with their dads or guy friends.

10.2.9.2 Full Boy Mode – non-hormonal

This is probably the most challenging thing for a trans boy after puberty. They use binders to completely hide their breasts. Try to suppress their estrogen production through strenuous exercise. They do their best to present entirely as a young man in every way. They even learn to add depth and growl to their voice by using chest resonance. This may be on a full-time or part-time basis, but each time they go out in guy-mode, they do everything they can to appear to be men.

This is the highest risk for many trans boys, but it also puts them as close as possible to transition therapy. In fact, by "coming out" in this way, they often find help getting access to the blockers and testosterone required to help them start the road to complete transition. Unfortunately, teens may still find it very difficult to get their mastectomy, which is a much more urgently needed procedure for them to pass. There is a real risk if they reach this point at 14 or 15.. Two to three years of extreme binding will cause severe bruising and damage. At that point, the mastectomy becomes a life-saving surgery. The bigger problem is that the inability to get the mastectomy can often lead to suicide or "accidents".

We'll talk about blockers and male hormones in a later section.

10.3 TRANS GIRL PUBERTY

The experiences of transgender girls are similar to those of transgender boys but with additional dimensions.

10.3.1 AWARENESS OF PUBERTY

Boys often figure out that they can pee standing up and women can't. Still, they don't truly understand the process of puberty until they are about 10 years old. For ordinary boys, this may take the form of becoming aware of erections and their first ejaculations. Since the signs are less visible, parents may not talk about puberty as early as they do with girls.

Transgender girls often panic when they understand that they will soon go through puberty. Before puberty, they are often excited that they can fit into the clothes of a mother or older sister. They are happy that the strict separation of boys in girls has eased. And then they learn about puberty.

The teacher explains the reproductive system in school, talking about testes and phallus. Many trans girls born with gender ambiguity may find it unusual. They don't have testicles yet, because they haven't dropped. It's not a question they want to ask in a class full of boys, especially boys who will be in the showers with them within the next 48 hours.

Then the teacher will start to talk about growing taller, shoulders getting broader, upper body getting stronger. They will talk about the growth of facial hair and body hair. The movie may even show a man with a dark facial "shadow" or beard. The lectures or films will talk about the Adam's apple, the drop of the voice, and ejaculations. There may even be a few minutes on the use of condoms, sexually transmitted diseases, and pregnancies. There will often be a discussion of the reproduction process with a 5-second reference to insemination, how the fertilized egg becomes an embryo, a fetus, then is born and becomes a baby.

To a transgender girl, these lessons are like telling her she will become a werewolf, sentenced to a life of isolation and solitude.

10.3.2 FEAR OF PUBERTY

To the trans girl, the prospect of growing so tall with such big feet that they could never fit in girl's clothes, having a big, pronounced Adam's apple bobbing up and down is bad enough. Singing bass and looking like Milton Berle in Camp Drag is their worst nightmares made a permanent reality.

Many trans boys will even have new nightmares as a result. At the same time, they may become even more desperate to prevent such a puberty from happening. It's not uncommon for trans girls to explore different ways to castrate themselves to prevent puberty.

Page 92 of 219

10.3.3 Early Signs of Puberty

The earliest signs and warnings of puberty are most often unexpected erections and ejaculation either in the form of "wet dreams" or as the result of arousal with or without masturbation. Before these warning signs, boys often experience erections in bed or when taking a bath or shower, touching themselves, or thinking about kissing a pretty girl or a handsome boy. However, they don't ejaculate.

10.3.4 The Testes Drop

The most dramatic and traumatic for a trans girl, especially if she has undescended testes, is when the testicles drop through the inguinal canal. Before this, they were so far up that there was no sensation of them. To a transgender girl who learns of testes before they drop, their hope is that they might have ovaries that are up inside them. They hope the phallus is just a mistake and will fall off or go away.

When the testes drop, often during a bath, the first urge of a trans girl is to try to push them back where they belong. When that fails, because it's so intensely painful, they can't continue, and they keep dropping down. The next question becomes, "How do I get rid of them?"

Before the 19th century, it was not uncommon for a boy at this point to have himself castrated. They could go to a shepherd, veterinarian, or even a doctor and have the testes removed. It was painful and was done in a matter of seconds. Even the opium mixed with 100 proof alcohol was not enough to dull the pain completely. After the first cut was made, the entire process took about 20 seconds. In fact, this type of castration of trans boys, turning them into eunuchs, has been common practice for over 10,000 years of recorded history.

There is archeological evidence that transgender eunuchs may have existed as far back as 30,000 years ago. The Hijra cult in India has existed for over ten thousand years. Their members usually came to them as boys before puberty. Once castrated, many cultures would put the eunuchs with the women, keeping the peace, forming relationships and friendships, helping the women, and learning the cultures and languages of a leader's many wives. Eunuchs often functioned as emissaries or "angels" in Greek, passing messages and negotiating on behalf of their masters.

Even into the late 19th century, feminine boys would often run away from abusive fathers and got recruited to work in brothels, voluntarily castrated to remain desirable and marketable into their 30s.

Many of the first "sex change" operations were made possible with the availability of anesthesia. It gave doctors the time to explore the process on willing subjects. Many patients raised funds to pay for the surgeries by working as models, actresses, singers, or in brothels.

To a modern transgender girl, pre-teen surgical castration is not an option, but they will try nonsurgical methods. Heat, such as boiling water, extreme cold such as dry ice, strangulation using rubber bands or string, or even attempting to crush them are not unusual. Still, unfortunately, they are almost always ineffective. Some of these methods do leave tell-tale scars that can be a red flag for doctors that there may be an issue, that this male patient may be a trans girl.

10.3.5 BODY HAIR

Body hair is often an early warning of puberty. This can be very traumatic for a trans girl. Even though the hair may still be relatively light, thin, and sparse, she will see herself turning into some ugly hairy beast growing fur. Other people see the light leg hair. She sees herself as Chewbacca, the Wookie, or the werewolf.

10.3.6 FACIAL HAIR

Facial hair is another kind of nightmare. As soon as it appears, the immediate urge is to get rid of it, shave it off, and make it go away forever. Of course, that only makes it thicker, darker, and courser. I've known trans girls who have tried depilatory creams intended for legs on their faces, often keep in on for so long that their faces were blistered, and yet the course male hair persisted.

Some transgender women will grow their beards to even a few inches long so they can wax them off. This is extremely painful and leaves scabs, blisters, and redness, but the hair that does grow back is thinner and lighter. Unfortunately, it takes several months to grow the hair each time. It's so painful that it becomes challenging to complete the process even once, let alone the multiple times required.

10.3.7 VOICE CHANGES

Perhaps one of the most dreaded changes is the voice changes. The Adam's Apple bobbing up and down on the neck and the voice breaking into a deep bass or even a low tenor voice can be incredibly upsetting to a transgender girl. This can often trigger suicide ideation because the voice change and visible apple can seem like "the point of no return."

10.3.8 BODY CHANGES

The other irreversible changes that can be extremely upsetting to a trans girl are the body changes. Shooting up to anywhere near six feet tall can upset any girl, but for a trans girl, it means being read more easily.

With the height comes the growth of the feet. If the boy's shoe size is size 10, the women's shoe size is 2 sizes larger, and pretty size 12 shoes are nearly impossible to find.

What makes these changes even worse is that they are irreversible.
Body hair can be waxed off. Facial hair can be removed with
electrolysis and laser. The Adam's Apple can be shaved. The vocal
cords can be shortened. But there isn't a way to shorten and narrow
someone's feet.

When trans girls develop an unmistakably masculine body and feel
that transition is no longer an option, they may explore magic and
reincarnation. Buddhists, Hindus, and many Native American
cultures believe in reincarnation. Christians believe in eternal life
even though death is still a reality. It may be possible that the soul
has eternal life by moving on to new bodies. Would that be an
alternative to heaven?

To the transgender girl, reincarnation may be her last hope. Often,
the one thing that will keep her from committing suicide
immediately, is learning about karma. Suppose they selfishly kill
themselves without giving something good back to humanity in this
life. They could end up as women in Africa, where tribes still
circumcise women. Or in China, where infant girls are killed or
"sent down" to become little more than enslaved people or sex
workers.

For some, this may be enough to keep them alive, and looking for
ways to help others at least enough to make their next life less
miserable than this one.

10.3.9 GAY COMMUNITY

Many trans girls find their initial support in the gay community.
They are seen as femme boys, and gay boys often feel safer coming
out to trans girls who appear "obviously gay".

Even if a trans girl is not attracted to boys, she can build an
excellent support network within the community. Possibly even
meet other trans girls who can help them in different ways. Giving
them referrals to therapists and doctors who are safe to talk to.

10.4 Non-binary Options

Just as the lesbian community provides non-binary options to trans boys, the gay community offers non-binary options to trans girls. In 21st century vocabulary, they are often called twinks. Boys who are obviously feminine and apparently gay. A trans girl might go to a gay club in clothes tailored to fit snugly or even wear women's jeans and blouses.

10.4.1 Crossdressing & Gender Fluid

Crossdressing is often a pressure relief valve for trans girls very early in their lives. Many trans girls will start crossdressing very privately soon after the bullying begins at school.

Not all crossdressers are trans girls, and many trans girls don't start dressing as girls until they start the early stages of transition.

Crossdressing is often very private since no partner is required. The dressing may start as only one or two items, such as panties and tights. It may take years to expand to full wardrobes, often because they don't have access to clothes that fit.

There's a critical distinction between cisgender crossdressers and transgender crossdressers. Cisgender crossdressers often dress only to be sexually aroused. They can't wait to get their clothes off after achieving gratification. A transgender girl will often delay gratification, spend more time dressed and keep the clothes on after reaching orgasm. Another distinction is that they are the girl in their fantasies if they are transgender.

Because crossdressing is so private, many crossdressers will keep their secret for years, even decades. I've read many accounts of crossdressers who have kept their secrets from their own wives for 20 years or more. Some even have elaborate hiding places for their "stash" of clothing, ranging from false bottom drawers to hidden compartments in the walls.

Page 97 of 219

Often, crossdressers are transgender, but they can't risk even hinting that they are transgender because they have invested so heavily in keeping their secret. Once they are discovered or come out as crossdressers, they often quickly realize that they are transgender and start their transition.

Part of the WPATH protocol is Real Life Experience (RLE). This includes being required to dress as a girl evenings and weekends as much as possible. Even sleeping in nighties or girls' PJs. One of the reasons for this is that crossdressers will lose the "thrill" of dressing as they do so all the time. As a result, cisgender crossdressers will stop the transition process because it's not as fun and exciting as they had hoped.

There are also many "late bloomers", trans girls profoundly repressed, bullied, terrorized, and shamed when they were very young. They have forced themselves to live as cisgender. Even though he ended up in a desk job, George Jorgensen was a marine. There have even been men in Special Forces who transitioned after retiring. For them, having a lover or girlfriend introduce them to crossdressing in a safe environment can awaken all those repressed feelings.

These initial explorations are like someone wearing good glasses for the first time for late bloomers. They didn't know they weren't seeing everything they should be seeing until after putting on the glasses. Suddenly they can see details they had never been able to see before.

At least half of all crossdressers are essentially gender fluid. While they are dressed in women's clothes, they want to be women. While dressed, they feel like they are women. They hate going back to men's clothes, at least until they are dressed as men again.

10.4.2 FEMME

In the gay community, trans girls are often accepted as femme. Other names have been used within the culture. Femmes, Folles, queens, and "Twinks".

Generally, these are young men who are very slender, dress to show off their form and skin and throw in feminine touches to their wardrobe. They might wear daisy dukes and a crop top, or a dress shirt tied above the waist.

In gay environments, such as gay bars & community centers, they will be more flamboyant and overtly feminine. Often, they come very close to being dressed as girls.

10.4.3 FLUID

Gender fluid is more common among trans girls in the gay community who need to present as men for work and interactions with clients, management, and vendors.

They can then go home and dress as feminine as they want and go to clubs and centers that cater to the LGBT community.

10.4.4 DRAG QUEEN

People often confuse trans girls with drag queens. Drag Queens are PERFORMERS who dress hyperfeminine. They lip-sync or sing, wearing enormous wigs, formal dresses with sequins, satin, or fur. They sing musical numbers of famous female icons like Cher, Madonna, and Marilyn Monroe. Others develop their own personalities.

However, at the end of the show, MOST of the performers take off the wigs, gowns, make-up, and false eyelashes, put on their boy clothes, and join their gay friends as a guy.

Some transgender women do perform in drag shows, and many are very good at it. At the end of their performance, they put on casual girl clothes. Then they might even hang out with lesbians or with gay friends who know that they are trans.

The most important thing to remember is that drag is performance art, not a lifestyle. It is rare to see a drag performer in full drag shopping at the local shopping mall on a Saturday afternoon.

10.4.5 QUEER

Queer or genderqueer also exists in the gay community. And like the lesbian community, queer men may or may not be trans girls. They can pick from the "menu" of male and female clothes, accessories, makeup, and mannerisms.

Queers may adjust their presentation to their situation. Turning the volume way up in a safe place with other gay men in the room and toning it way down at the local Denney's.

For transgender women, this is an excellent way to begin to be authentic without being blatant about it or committing to transition. It's a way to avoid upsetting parents, going out looking more like a guy, then making a few changes in the car to glam up.

For many, being queer is a very comfortable space, and they may stay there for years. For many trans girls, being queer is a rest-stop on the way to transition.

10.5 BINARY OPTIONS

Most transgender girls' ultimate dream is to fully transition to be beautiful women like they see in the magazines. Or even like one of the pretty girls in their school.

Unfortunately, contrary to popular myth and misinformation, it's not like a 14-year-old trans girl can walk into the doctor's office and say, "Make me a girl now." Even adults can't get the hormones and surgery "on-demand". Adults can get hormones and blockers after reading a large document, listening to the lecture given by the doctor, and signing an "Informed Consent" form. Minors have to follow the WPATH standards of care milestones.

The closest to an "all in one" visit is taking a trip to Thailand. In one trip, you can get vaginoplasty, labiaplasty, liposuction, and breast augmentation. Of course, you must get back to the United States. You'll need either a passport with a female name or a passport and a therapist's letter explaining that you are transgender.

There are still prerequisites before such an "all in one" trip. Electrolysis of the genitals and surrounding area. A BMI below 28, and good general health. Doctors recommend waiting for at least 2 years of HRT to take effect. By then, the breast growth will have slowed enough to be predictable.

Furthermore, this "package" is only performed on Americans old enough to legally consent, age 18 or older.

10.5.1 REAL-LIFE EXPERIENCE (RLE)

One of the prerequisites for any form of intervention is to begin the real-life experience. If this is started before puberty, the doctor will check blood levels for a sudden increase in testosterone before starting blockers. Only AFTER this spike will blockers be initiated.

During the real-life experience, the trans girl will need to see a therapist to demonstrate socialization skills and networking skills. Preparing them for transition to full-time safely by living at least half time, including evenings and weekends.

For a trans girl who has already been living full-time at school and at home and already has a network of 10-12 friends in her school, getting approval for hormones can be done more quickly.

Page 101 of 219

The therapist will require more visits for trans girls who haven't started living as girls. A therapist will coach the trans girl through many different exercises. Starting from simple but terrifying, such as walking to the mailbox and back as a girl at night. Getting into the car and driving around the block. The assignments get more complex over time. Going to a convenience store and buying a soda. Going to a movie theater, going to a shopping mall in another neighborhood, going to a shopping mall nearby. Going to support groups, and LGBT centers for support group meetings and other activities based on talents, abilities, and interests.

These exercises don't just build confidence. They also facilitate a safe and successful transition. They ALSO help transgender girls determine if they are ready to transition at this stage of their lives.

10.5.2 FULL GIRL MODE – NON-HORMONAL

Teen trans girls can generally stay on blockers until about 16 years old without starting hormones. In the UK, NHS recommends starting hormones at age 16. In the USA, the standard is to begin hormones at age 14 or after 1 year on blockers, whichever is later. These are general guidelines.

Doctors give more detailed guidance based on kidney function, baseline hormone levels, and impact on heart rate, weight, and blood pressure. This helps determine how much a patient needs and how it should be administered. I started on pills, switched to shots when my estrogen levels dropped and switched to a patch when my heart rate got too low.

For trans girls who have not started hormones, there are some options to help them be able to live as girls full-time or part-time.

Breast forms of an appropriate size can provide natural-looking breasts. During the summer, school-age trans girls can even use an adhesive, a surgical glue, to keep them placed for several weeks at a time.

Gaffs are a particular type of underwear that makes it easy to "tuck" and keep boy bits placed so that they are invisible. Even in a swimsuit, it's nearly impossible to see anything even remotely male. There are even some gaffs that are molded on the outside to look like the folds of labia. These can even be configured with the ability to pee while tucked. The most important thing is that these gaffs prevent erections.

Waxing is a common and popular way to get rid of body hair for men and women. Many transgender girls only need to be waxed about 5 times, and they will often not need to shave much, if at all, after that.

If puberty has started and arrested, it is often necessary to perform electrolysis. This is a painful process that involves inserting a stylus into a hair follicle, applying an electrical current, and then pulling the hair out down to the root.

After puberty, male facial hair has 4-5 times thicker and longer roots than female facial hair. Electrolysis, zapping and plucking these thick hairs by the roots, can be extremely painful. This procedure is only done by licensed professionals in many states, including medically supervised anesthesia. A four-hour session that can remove all the facial hair for one growth cycle and includes anesthesia costs about $400 per session. Usually, five sessions are needed over a 12-to-18-month period. Another round of five sessions may be necessary to entirely remove the hair

A common problem with "home electrolysis" kits and programs can be scarring of the face. Suppose the operator tries to zap a pore instead of a follicle. In that case, the result is the destruction of the pores and permanent scars. On the flip side, too much electrolysis can result in a "shiny" look that makes the skin almost look like plastic. This can result in being "read" as a transgender woman.

Before opposing blockers, adult men should try an hour of electrolysis to realize what not having them can mean for their children. The women detractors should watch. It's something one wouldn't wish on their worst enemy, let alone their own child.

10.5.3 FULL GIRL MODE – HORMONES

Hormones are administered only to transgender women under strict medical supervision, regardless of age. This includes blockers and hormones.

For transgender girls, the most used blocker is Spironolactone, originally used as a diuretic to help control blood pressure by lowering sodium levels and raising potassium levels. Male patients hated it because they lost their ability to get erections and ejaculate. To a cisgender man, this is a very upsetting condition. Doctors ran blood tests on these patients and discovered that the patient's testosterone levels had dropped to the levels typical for a cisgender woman.

Before Spironolactone, the typical hormone treatment was to saturate the trans girl with enough estrogen to suppress testosterone production and produce the effects of female puberty. The problem was that this much estrogen, especially in some of its early synthetic forms, or animal estrogens such as Premarin, could produce deadly blood clots. In the 20s and 30s, girls getting massive doses of injected estrogen were dying of strokes. Even some trans women in the United States treated with massive estrogen doses died of blood clots. Clots went to the heart or brain, causing heart attacks or strokes.

Spironolactone allows the doctor to use only a fraction of the estrogen to produce the necessary effects. In addition, the development of bioidentical estrogen, called estradiol, has made hormone treatments much safer. Ironically, for transgender women, the lack of erections, shrinking of the genitalia, and lack of ejaculations during orgasm is a BENEFIT to most trans girls. When you consider these side effects, fears that a transgender woman on blockers might sexually assault a cisgender woman in a locker room or bathroom seems almost comical.

Initially, physicians will start a patient on the Spironolactone pills to help them determine the minimum effective dose. They can switch to either injections or implants. Blood tests are taken as frequently as once a month. No less than once a quarter for the first year.

The same is valid with estradiol. Initially, the doctor will recommend pills because they are the easiest to take and administer. Unfortunately, about 80-90% of the estradiol taken orally is processed by the liver and doesn't make it to the bloodstream. As a result, only about 10% makes it to the bloodstream. Pills can be continued until the liver starts processing even more of what is taken. The liver and kidneys reduce the body's bloodstream levels of oral estrogen over time.

Eventually, the doctor will switch to injections or dermal patches, which allow far less estrogen to be used in a way that emulates the regular cycles of women's estrogen cycles. Even with pills, it is common for trans women to experience peaks and valleys and even have the emotional symptoms of periods, including irritability and crying jags. Some of us love to watch Disney movies and cry many happy tears. This is one of the reasons why WPATH recommends a therapist or social worker.

10.5.4 ANCIENT HISTORY HORMONES

As mentioned earlier, history has shown that transgender women existed and often had themselves castrated before puberty. There was an ancient form of hormone therapy as well. The urine of pregnant animals such as mares, cows, nanny goats, and ewes was collected, dried, mixed with wine, and consumed as a drink. The most potent and easily collected was pregnant mare urine, primarily because mares aren't usually milked for extended periods. Even today, this is packaged as a drug called Premarin, which is still used for women after menopause.

A common problem among many trans girls on a budget or unhelpful doctors is taking plant estrogens called phytoestrogens. These may have some benefits for a woman in early menopause. Still, they are useless for a trans girl with functioning testicles. Taking enough to get any real help can be even more dangerous than taking too much estradiol. A waste of money for transgender girls. Without blockers or castration, the testosterone outvotes the estrogen.

11 ACUTE GENDER DYSPHORIA

Acute Gender Dysphoria is a condition caused by the combination of being transgender and being FORCED to live as cisgender. It is a potentially FATAL disease with exceptionally high mortality and morbidity rates. Those suffering from untreated Acute Gender Dysphoria have a very short life expectancy, with an increased risk of dying of suicide or accident before they are 25 years old. The ONLY successful treatment for Acute Gender Dysphoria is a successful transition.

Historically, there have been many names for this malady, which were misleading and counterproductive. In the early 20th Century, it was termed Gender Identity Psychosis. Freud observed that many women wished they were men and called it "penis envy". He determined that it was pretty ordinary. However, when he also observed that many male patients wanted to be women, he assumed they must suffer from psychosis. Treatment often included those like treatments for hysteria. Later, Robert Galbraith Heath and Bill Masters added anal rape with painfully large objects, beatings, isolation, sleep deprivation, and lobotomy. Many of the intermediate treatments were more a matter of curiosity or sadistic interest since nearly all of those diagnosed with Gender Identity Psychosis ultimately had to be lobotomized to prevent them from killing themselves at the first opportunity.

In the latter half of the 20th century, the DSM changed it to Gender Identity Disorder (GID). The problem with this terminology is that it still presumed that the problem was Gender Identity. So, it might be possible to use brainwashing and MK-Ultra mind control techniques. Perhaps they could somehow brainwash a transgender person into being a cisgender person or make a gay man straight.

Treatments for GID included electric shock, insulin shock, aversion therapy, including chemically induced fear, nausea, or pain while being forced to watch erotic movies. The book and movie "A Clockwork Orange" very accurately describe techniques routinely used in the United States to try to cure both men and women suffering from Gender Dysphoria and homosexuality. Unfortunately, almost invariably, those treated had to be lobotomized because they would kill themselves within weeks of being released.

In the late 20th century, especially in the 1970s, GID was treated with massive doses of Haldol. This was the chemical equivalent of a lobotomy. It eliminated the costs of institutionalization and provided at least a few months between discharge and suicide. By the late 1980s, therapists realized that people with GID who didn't transition before their 25th birthday would most likely be dead before their 30th birthday. Nearly 90% of those "talked out of" transitioning ended up dead, often with no warning, no note, and no clear indication of suicide or accident.

Sadly, there are still attempts to associate gender dysphoria with psychosis indirectly. There hasn't even been a serious effort to determine cause and effect. Chronic stress from daily assaults and threats, molestation, incest or rape by sexual predators, and prostitution for survival are known factors leading to psychosis. Gender Identity and Gender Dysphoria are not the cause of psychosis.

This is why a therapist trained in treating Gender Dysphoria must determine whether additional trauma needs to be addressed. A trans girl may be an alcoholic and have acute gender dysphoria. Both conditions need to be addressed, but not one or the other. Refusing to treat Gender Dysphoria might eliminate the motivation to quit drinking and even result in worse binges.

11.1 TRANS BOY

Acute Gender Dysphoria (GD) manifests itself in many different ways. It often results in many dangerous and even life-threatening results. Even when the results aren't fatal, they are often expensive to treat.

11.1.1 HARD BINDING

One of the most dramatic and blatant expressions of GD is damage to the breasts resulting from extreme binding. Often binding materials can include ace bandages, sports tape, medical tape, duct tape, and even bondage tape. Bindings are so tight that breasts aren't visible at all. The bindings are often worn for days at a time, even during showers. They will get themselves excused from gym class so they won't have to shower with girls, and they will lock the bathroom door, so their parents won't see the bindings.

The problem is that such extreme binding causes bruising, cists, even gangrene. Many trans men have a hard time looking upset when the doctor tells them that they will lose their breasts.

11.1.1.1 Muscle Development

Many trans men have discovered that they can significantly suppress estrogen production through extreme exercise. Heavy-duty boot-camp style workouts with excessive heart rates can reduce estrogen blood levels and result in better health. The heart rates go to the high extremes. There are increased risks of life-threatening conditions. This includes embolisms resulting from extreme heart rates and blood pressure.

11.1.2 SELF-MEDICATION

A bigger problem and much greater risk is self-medication. Sadly, getting hormones without medical supervision is dangerous medically and can also lead to dark places legally.

11.1.2.1 OTC Virility Builders

Several "food supplements" offer "testosterone boost" are sold in stores like GNC, Walgreens, CVS, and big box stores. Unfortunately, most of these are not actually testosterone. They are compounds that help a male body with testes to produce more testosterone. The problem is that this is not clear. A trans boy may increase dosages to dangerous levels that cause other hazardous side effects such as diabetes or hypertension.

11.1.2.2 Mail Order

There are ways to get actual testosterone via mail-order, and often the only requirement is a credit card. The problem with this is that it's easy to get impurities, animal testosterone, or synthetics that don't do anything without medical supervision. Taking too much testosterone can cause hypertension, heart problems, and worse.

11.1.2.3 Black Market Testosterone

Black Market Testosterone is a dark market not significantly different from buying and selling illegal drugs. The drugs sold are often in vials. The vials may be diluted or have addictive drugs added to create a dependency. Failing a blood test because your black-market testosterone dealer added some meth can be a real problem. Especially if you are trying to get a security clearance or work for a bank.

11.2 TRANS GIRL

Transgender girls with Acute Gender Dysphoria (GD) often seek out the historical solution of castration. Many know that their dog gets fixed, so he won't mark the rug, and they understand the concept of castration. They can learn about agriculture, animal husbandry, and castration methods by going to the library. Of course, if they try to go to a veterinarian and ask to be castrated, they will be rebuffed soundly.

11.2.1 SELF-CASTRATION ATTEMPTS

There are rare examples of transgender girls trying to surgically castrate themselves. Some of these girls are as young as 10 years old. Attempts at surgical castration seldom go well. They are clearly an act of desperation. Too often, the initial cut is made and the first one removed, and then a 911 call is placed in hopes that the paramedics will arrive in time. Even if one testicle is removed. No attempt is made to remove the other. Instead, she may find herself locked up in a psychiatric ward for days or months at a time.

Much more common and much less reported are the non-surgical methods. The reasoning is that they can't remove their testicles by themselves, but they can try to render them nonfunctional. Essentially, the thinking is to try to destroy them while they are on the inside.

A technique used to castrate sheep is to use thick rubber bands to cut off circulation. Eventually, the testes just die, shrivel up, and the bands fall off. Some transgender girls have tried this, but one of the problems is that walking on two legs provides circulation, and the testes don't shrivel as expected. Another method is tying them tight with string or thread, again tight enough to cut off circulation. This is not a particularly effective method and can become very painful, even dangerous.

Boiling or freezing are also theoretically noteworthy options. Unfortunately, pouring boiling water or dry ice on the scrotum will cause burns to the skin. It's painful but will not do long-term damage sufficient to function as castration. The bigger problem is the scars, blisters, and burns to the scrotum.

11.2.2 SELF-MEDICATION

Another serious risk of Acute Gender Dysphoria is self-medication. Some of the issues with this are FAR MORE dangerous for transgender women than the options available to transgender boys.

Page 111 of 219

11.2.2.1 Phytoestrogens

Phytoestrogens are often referred to as "Plant Estrogens". These are natural forms of estrogen that are often used by premenopausal women. They are NOT a substitute for bioidentical estradiol. The most significant risk when transgender girls try to take phytoestrogens is that they will keep increasing the dosage. They reach dangerous levels to get the desired effects such as breasts, fat distribution, and facial feminization. The problem is that phytoestrogens do not suppress testosterone production, and even at the bottom of the male range, testosterone outvotes estrogen.

Without a testosterone blocker, taking phytoestrogens is just throwing money down the toilet.

11.2.2.2 Mail-order Hormones

A transgender girl ordering mail-order hormones is VERY Dangerous, especially since there is no medical supervision. Taking too much spironolactone can cause dangerous dehydration, dramatic drops in blood pressure, and dangerously slow heart rates. I knew one transgender girl who had been taking medically supervised spironolactone, and her blood pressure had dropped to 90/60. Her heart rate had dropped to 38 BPM. A teen transgender girl in a rush could easily accidentally kill herself without even realizing that's what she was doing.

Mail-order Estradiol isn't much better. Again, an overly eager teen transgender girl could start taking so much estrogen that they develop blood clots. This can cause future heart problems and strokes in a few years or even earlier.

Unfortunately, there is no medical supervision, and the warning signs won't be discovered until it's too late.

11.2.2.3 Black-market Hormones

Black Market Hormones are also treacherous. Often, the dealers of black-market hormones do silicone parties and other "filling" parties where silicone gel is injected directly into lips, face, breasts, and hips. They may also deal in amphetamines to help the girls lose weight (and get hooked). Some of these dealers are also recruiters for prostitution rings.

11.3 THE FINAL SOLUTION – SUICIDE

Depending on the survey, the suicide attempt rate for transgender women is between 40% and 50% of all respondents. No word from those who were dead and couldn't respond.

There are at least 1.4 million transgender people in the United States. An average of roughly 16,000 teens aged 12 to 19 die of suicide or accidents every year. Not all accidents are accidents.

11.3.1 IDEATION

Stage 1 is the **"ideation"** stage. A depressed person finds themself thinking about suicide more and more. However, the fear of suicide still outweighs its attraction. The person may be thinking dark thoughts ("my family would be better off without me"). Obsessing over dark music (i.e., repeatedly playing the same depressing song). Expressing thoughts of death, suicide, pain, and hopelessness through artistic expression. They have not yet begun to formulate a specific plan. People in Stage 1 are not imminently lethal. Many are involuntarily hospitalized for expressing thoughts of suicide in this stage. Psychotherapy with a well-trained behavioral health provider is highly effective and encouraged in this stage. Without adequate treatment, ideation may last indefinitely or escalate to Stage 2.

For a transgender person, ideation is often triggered when confronted with the belief or argument that transition will not be permitted or successful. Being told it would not be physiologically possible. Being told that the transition would not be successful even if they changed. Being told they will not be accepted as a woman. This includes the discovery that the cost of the procedures required to produce a successful transition is too high. So high they are perceived to be impossible.

It is often at this point that transgender people begin to consider the possibility of reincarnation, of the beliefs of eastern religions. They see suicide as their last and only hope of getting a body that they can accept. A transgender boy hopes he can be reincarnated as a boy, and a transgender girl hopes she can be reincarnated as a girl.

11.3.2 PLANNING

Stage 2 is the "**planning**" stage, during which the person's dark thoughts begin to formulate a specific suicide plan. Friends and family may notice the person's depression worsening. Their loved one begins to withdraw from touching others or being touched by others. They may stop verbalizing their pain and suffering while seeming to be in more pain than ever. People in Stage 2 are not imminently lethal, although they critically need effective psychological care. Stage 2 rarely lasts longer than several months because it is psychologically painful. The person feels compelled to decide to die (thus moving into Stage 3) or not to die at that time, which most people do not discuss with loved ones. They often wrestle with it in isolation.

Transgender people are often very creative, and they often have compassion for certain people in their lives. They may do the research on dozens of different methods. There was a television series called 1001 ways to die. Some were quite gruesome, but several were ways to make a suicide look like an accident. Transgender people often develop a distrust of mental health professionals. Especially if professionals have tried to deter them from transition. They don't want to take any chance to be institutionalized if they survive an attempt.

11.3.3 DECISION

Stage 3 begins when the suicidal person makes the decision to die. The moment the decision is made, it goes "unconscious", and the person goes on "auto-pilot". People in Stage 3 are eminently lethal. However, they seem more "normal" than they have seemed in a long time. At this point, the depression appears to suddenly lift. This is because the person has decided to die and is no longer wrestling with the decision.

11.3.4 IMPLEMENTATION

Unfortunately, most mental health professionals and family members do not recognize "auto-pilot". They breathe a sigh of relief because their patient seems so much better. They don't realize that the client is on a collision course with suicide. People on "auto-pilot" typically attempt suicide within the next 48 hours. Be alert when a depressed patient who doesn't seem to improve after weeks or months of therapy suddenly appears to get much better for no reason.

11.3.5 ATTEMPT

Remember that transgender teens are often careful to make sure that their suicide does NOT look like a suicide. As a result, if they combine a bunch of drugs and alcohol during a party and don't die of the overdose, it will be treated as an accidental overdose. They had just had too much to drink, or maybe somebody put something in their drink. In the 60s, there were a lot of kids who did acid and decided they could fly and jumped off a building. How many of those flights were suicides treated as drug-induced hallucinations?

Transgender suicides often take creative forms, stepping in front of a truck while wearing black hoody and sweatpants. Getting into a fight with bikers or cowboys and laughing at them as they hit you and kick you, provoking them to do something fatal. You aren't defending yourself. Taking a combination of prescription, over-the-counter, and recreational drugs in combination makes it harder to figure out how to give you an antidote in time. It can also make it harder for people to realize that you are not just drunk. Losing your balance on your bicycle will make it look like an accident. Sitting on the bridge's handrail across the interstate and falling backward makes it look like you just lost your balance while resting. Even more effective if you're drunk and high.

One of the leading causes of teen deaths is traffic accidents. How many of those accidents are suicides? Very hard to tell, especially if the person driving was alone and transgender.

11.3.6 SURVIVAL

Surviving a suicide attempt does not guarantee that there won't be another attempt. Transgender teens often plan their suicide attempts so that if they survive, they won't be institutionalized, committed, or otherwise prevented from making a future attempt.

Page 116 of 219

For this reason, they will often pick a time and place where it won't be noticed if they are sick or need to sleep for a few days. A vacation, business trip, staying at the dorm for a holiday, or a long weekend can all be dangerous times.

11.3.7 FATALITY

Because of these survival plans, there are often few clues that a transgender teen was transgender or that their death was a suicide. They may leave clues, such as wearing underwear of the opposite sex or even pictures of themselves in their preferred gender role, but no note.

Often, families will want police to report the death as an accident even when it is obviously a suicide. This may address the religious concerns of the parent who sees suicide as a mortal sin. Suicide means they can't be buried in the cemetery of their religion. Even the children would be damned. They desire to avoid any further investigation into the motives behind the suicide.

There can be indicators that the victim was transgender are blatantly obvious. A corpse that is fully cross-dressed, tucked, and signs of bootleg hormones. The police will often honor the request of the parents that the transgender status of the victim not be included in police reports. Nor in statements to any reporters or investigators. Life insurance policies may not pay off on suicides but will pay double for accidental deaths.

The cover-up of transgender suicides often indicates that the parents were aware of an issue in many ways. They were aware that the child was suffering from acute dysphoria and did nothing to get the proper help. The parents may have even tried to force a child into conversion therapy in some cases. In effect, the suicide was a murder in which the victim was driven to end their own lives.

12 DISORIENTATION

This section discusses some of the critical drivers of Acute Gender Dysphoria. Disorientation occurs when a transgender person is discovered to be transgender, and the response is hostility and danger.

12.1 DISCOVERY

Discovery can happen in any number of ways. The transgender girl is caught by a family member wearing the clothes of his mother or a sister. The transgender boy whose parents see him in his bindings or binder. A romantic interest hinting at the transgender behavior and the laugh that gives it away.

The discovery is with someone who trusts, expects, and accepts the transgender identity in the best possible world. The girlfriend likes that her boyfriend wants to be a girl. The lesbian was hoping that her girlfriend wanted to be a boy. Or the mother who has suspected for years but was afraid to ask because they were afraid their son would be upset about being asked if he was a "sissy".

Far too often, though, this first discovery can be terrifying and traumatizing. The father flies into a rage and beats his son for being a "sissy faggot". The girl pretended to be in love, then outs him to the football team.

12.2 INVOLUNTARY OUTING

The most problematic kind of outing is the involuntary outing. The malicious sister catches her brother in her clothes. She takes some pictures and immediately posts them to her Facebook, Twitter, and Snapchat accounts. It doesn't matter who makes this discovery. The instant exposure can be hazardous and even fatal. It can make the "bashing" worse than it has ever been. Gender Dysphoria becomes so Acute that it can trigger suicide attempts within days.

This type of "mass outing" is essentially murder.

12.3 SHAMING PUBLIC ATTACKS

The person making the discovery will often wait for the most strategic timing to make their attack as public as possible. Announcing it at the family Thanksgiving Dinner. Giving the Barbie Doll or skimpy lingerie at the big family Christmas gathering. Following this with pictures, recorded confessions, or videos can absolutely destroy any chance of family support. The homophobes and transphobes in the group will start going off.

Often, public shaming is timed for the most hostile audience possible. The family is at the church youth class. The youth pastor is ranting about the evils of homosexuality. That's when their sister tells everybody how much of a faggot her brother is. Or getting together with the football team, joking about some feminine boy, then making the discovery public when the jocks are all fired up and feeling particularly hateful.

It takes a special kind of sociopath to make this kind of attack. Still, often, the person making the revelation no longer even sees the transgender person as a person. Instead, they see her as a thing, something evil, a monster, even a thing to be destroyed.

Page 119 of 219

12.4 REJECTION BY FRIENDS

When the person making the discovery is a friend, this can be less damaging, but the loss of the friendship can be painful. It can make it more difficult to share their secret with others. Having your closest friend for years suddenly cut calls short, evade invitations, and stop making invitations, can be painful. To a transgender person, it can be a message that it isn't safe to tell ANY of your friends.

12.5 REJECTION BY ROMANTIC INTEREST

Romantic interests are the one group of people who really need to know. A transgender girl may be visibly feminine even while presenting as male. His girlfriend may see him as a lovely boy with extraordinary patience and a great sense of humor. Still, suppose he comes out to her as transgender. In that case, she may become extremely hostile at the thought of being a lesbian with her transgender girlfriend.

It's painful when someone you love rejects you suddenly and completely. This is especially true after spending weeks or months building the relationship. Trying to reach the point of trusting this person with your deepest secret. Still, it can be much worse when she suddenly starts telling all of her friends about what a "pervert" you are. Even if one of her friends might actually be interested in you BECAUSE you are transgender, they know they would out themselves if they approached you. Her friend has made it unsafe to do so.

The worst-case scenario is when love turns to hate, and the love interest makes it a point to make your life as miserable as they can. They will expose you to the most homophobic and transphobic groups at school and laugh as you are tormented.

12.6 PARENTAL REJECTION OF TEENS

Perhaps the worst possible form of rejection is when one or both parents reject their child for being transgender. At first, this may just be dismissal. "It's just a phase. You'll grow out of it." Then it becomes avoidance "I don't want to talk about it, don't bring it up again." Then it becomes denial. "You're not a girl. You're just crazy. We'll get someone to straighten you out." Usually followed by attempts at conversion therapy. And finally, flat out rejection "If you want to be I girl, then here are some dresses, go find someone who wants you!"

12.7 REJECTION BY FAMILY

Rejection is a severe problem for transgender kids, especially since it usually happens to kids at their most rebellious stage, around 13 years old. This is not a good time to be on the street with nothing but a duffle bag full of girl's clothes for the transgender girl or a bag full of boy's clothes for the transgender boy.

12.7.1 HOMELESSNESS

One in five transgender people will experience homelessness in their lifetime, often soon after coming out and being rejected by their families. They often have no home, no other family, no money, and usually only the clothes on their back. To make matters worse, they have often been abused by one or both of their parents, boys in school, and have few friends and few, if any, adults they trust.

13 SURVIVAL TACTICS

They may try a homeless shelter for men and find that their true gender comes through. Sometimes there are giveaways such as plucked eyebrows, pierced ears, long hair that has been styled in a feminine way. Or transgender boys, hair that has been cut exceptionally short in a masculine style. Transgender girls are often the victims of violence and sexual assault in men's shelters. Safer shelters like Salvation Army turn transgender kids away. Because they are "obviously gay" or visibly transgender. Women's shelters turn them away even when they are visibly feminine. Transgender boys are turned away from women's shelters because they are too butch. They are turned away from church-oriented places. They get attacked in public "all gender" shelters because they are told to sleep closer to the men.

Transgender kids in shelters are also more likely to have their few remaining possessions stolen. This often leaves them with nothing after just a few days, not even a warm coat. There have even been incidents of transgender kids freezing to death on park benches just yards from the door of a shelter that turned them away.

HOMELESS LGBTQ YOUTH

An estimated 320,000 to 400,000 LGBTQ youth face homelessness in the United States each year.

LGBTQ youth experience many hardships, but perhaps one of the biggest is homelessness.

42% of homeless agencies do not address LGBTQ issues despite these elevated rates of homelessness.

40% of homeless youth are LGBTQ.

14.4 The average age that lesbian and gay youth in New York become homeless.

13.5 The average age that transgender youth in New York become homeless.

68% of homeless LGBTQ youth have experienced family rejection.

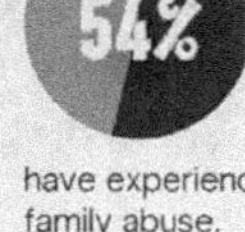

54% have experienced family abuse.

$53,665 The estimated cost to incarcerate a youth for one year.

$5,887 The estimated cost to permanently move a homeless youth off the streets and prevent them from becoming incarcerated.

Nearly 1 in 3 transgender people have been turned away from shelters.

15% of homeless shelters reported that helping homeless LGBTQ youth is "not central to their mission."

transstudent.tumblr.com
facebook.com/transstudent
twitter.com/transstudent

Take action at:
transstudent.org/homelessness

TSER
Trans Student Educational Resources

Design by Landyn Pan

13.1 COUCH HOPPING

Sometimes, homeless kids will try to contact kids from their school
or social groups to get a safe place to sleep. This might be a guest
room, but more often is a spare couch with someone they know.
This is a very temporary solution and often only provides temporary
shelter for a few weeks at most.

13.2 SURVIVAL SEX

Often, transgender teens are identified by predators and pimps, who
spot them from the feminine traits. They use this to entice them by
offering a safe place to live, food, and help to be feminine. This is
often a temptation that a transgender girl is desperate to believe.
Some of the recruiters are women, others are men. They offer help
with makeup, wardrobe, and beauty treatments that make them
visibly feminine. They even encourage them to dress sexy. At first,
this is just in exchange for sex, often in the pretext of a romantic
relationship. Then the money "runs out," and the transgender girl
needs to "earn her keep" to help with rent and more.

13.3 PROSTITUTION & SEX WORK

Whether recruited through survival sex or directly into prostitution,
the male or female recruiters will support them in dressing and
acting like a girl, even providing bootleg hormones. These
transgender girls are pimped to a specialized market that likes young
girls or young boys, primarily for oral and anal sex. A transgender
girl has been denied parental support. Many have been subjected to
conversion therapy. Getting the help of anyone to dress, act, and live
as a girl is like a dream come true. At first, their "dates" may be
selected from the least violent and repulsive. After a while, things
get ugly. Many tricks get rough after they've had their fun. They
beat the girl to alleviate guilt and shame for having sex with a "lady-
boy."

The sex can get more bizarre, including getting tied up. Dominants, sadists, and some scary customers may not honor safe words. Furthermore, safety measures such as check-up calls aren't made. A girl who is underproducing can end up being kidnapped, or worse.

13.4 PLAYERS AND MANIPULATORS

Part of the game, especially for transgender women, is the manipulators. Recruiters know how to identify transgender girls when they are most vulnerable. They may offer romance and the opportunity to dress and look like girls. It's a dream come true, and often their partner is a girl or guy only slightly older and experienced in this game. They get them dressed and feeling pretty. Help them get black market blockers and hormones, and often give them dangerous dosages with no medical supervision. They also try to make them even more submissive and compliant by being their domme, mistress, or master.

13.5 ROUGH TRADE/S&M/B&D

When they are ready to be "turned out," the girls may even be sold for cash to a pimp. Dominance and submission are common themes in transgender fiction, especially for transgender girls. Common themes include forced cross-dressing, forced hormones, and even male chastity devices, along with "pegging." With a strap-on, if the dominant is a woman. Oral and anal sex if the dominant is a man.

Of course, there's a big difference between fantasy and reality. Between rough sex, you both enjoy, and rape. The victim of rape has no control over the attack. No knowledge of what is likely to happen next. There is no discussion of hard and soft limits. No discussion of turn-offs.

A transgender girl is trained to enjoy sex with the more attractive clients. Before long, she's getting the fat guys, the mean guys, the guys who don't shower for days beforehand, and guys who beat up girls when they are done.

Page 125 of 219

13.6 BEING TRAFFICKED

Streetwalking transgender girls are scarce, and only a very few go this way. Most are marketed via the Internet. The girls are advertised as "models." They go to the engagement for a photoshoot. With the opportunity to earn "tips" or "extra on the side." Transgender girls willing to cut the picture taking short and go straight to the "extras" on the clock often get rewarded. Girls who only want to pose for pictures quickly find themselves with "rough trade" customers.

Other transgender girls get gigs as exotic dancers. The understanding is that they WILL do side-work after their time on stage. The girls do it because they can raise enough for breast implants and make more as topless dancers and provide anal sex.

Ironically, the pimps often do NOT want them to get "bottom surgery." No matter how much a girl might wish to get bottom surgery, they are only an exotic commodity as "T-Girls." Only as long as they are willing to play to the fetish fantasies of their clients.

13.7 ADDICTIONS

Like cisgender girls, transgender girls are often controlled with drugs. This includes the pimp's control of the hormones and blockers and pain pills for any plastic surgery such as breast enlargement. Of course, there are recreational drugs as well.

Often, transgender teens get addicted while they are still living at home. To numb the pain of gender dysphoria. Booze, pot, opiates, and sedatives are common drugs for going numb. Pimps prefer their girls wide awake and ready to work, so they use speed, coke, crack, and other stimulants. This also helps with weight control. Unfortunately, these drugs play hell with the body, resulting in a quick burn-out. Many runaway transgender girls have a short life expectancy. Sadly, murdered hookers don't get investigated either.

13.8 BLACKMAIL & CON GAMES

This is another ugly side. Recruiters and manipulators can often use photographs and videos to blackmail transgender girls and clients. A transgender girl can usually be manipulated into cooperation even while still at home by people who offer to help them dress up. Then they take pictures and then threaten to send images to their homophobic, transphobic parents or publish them.

If they stop cooperating, the manipulator will send the pictures to the parents and wait for the girl to be thrown out. Then they swoop in to "rescue" their victim.

On the flip side, transgender girls often work in rooms with lots of hidden cameras. Their pimps can get lots of pictures and videos of their clients. From many angles, including face, body, and the transgender girl's "extra equipment." For "tranny chasers" who don't want anyone knowing that they like transgender girls, the blackmail can be very effective but also very dangerous for the working girl.

14 HOPE

Transgender kids, especially transgender girls, often find hope in literature. It was the only source of even remotely accurate information on cross-dressing, transsexuality, or gender identity for decades. It was found on the "fine print" articles that most men don't read when looking for naked women's pictures. Pornography or "erotic literature." Transgender fiction can be found in popular magazines, adult magazines, and books.

14.1 THE SISSY FANTASY

The most common theme in fiction stories is sissy fantasy. These are stories with plots based on the feminization of a reluctant victim, often an alpha male who abuses women and gets forced into girls' clothes, but there are many variations.

14.1.1 FEMINIZATION STORIES

The sweetest and rarest form is the first-time feminization. These stories often have a caring partner, a friend, girlfriend, or wife who flirts and asks the person to be feminized to put on certain things. Depending on the length of the story, a short story may go directly to having their wife fully dress them. The couple goes out to the hotel bar or club and has some fun that may involve one or two other men. In long stories, the wife may slowly ease him into more feminine clothing until he is finally fully dressed and then shared. Most of these stories are written by men. It shows in their writing, their description of colors, fashion, and activities.

14.1.2 FORCED FEMINIZATION

Forced feminization differs from first-time feminization. The victim has usually lost a bet. Or has been blackmailed into cooperating. Or is otherwise forced to cooperate with their feminization. Often the victim is a wannabe alpha male who disrespects women, takes them for granted, or otherwise tries to dominate and exploit them. Many of these stories are written for and by feminist cisgender women. In fact, the feminist message is often woven into the story. The victim is often reduced to being a secretary or maid stripped of all previous rank and status. The women are often elevated to executive positions. Some of these can have a lot of hostility and abuse. Still, transgender girls, who don't see themselves as alpha males, often identify with the women. They worry most about how hard it would be to appear to be an unwilling victim.

14.1.3 PARAPHILIA

The third common theme beyond forced feminization is stories involving dressing, bondage, male chastity devices, denial, teasing, and being "milked" by using anal stimulation of the prostate. Ironically, this is a popular theme among transgender girls who take blockers and hormones. Many transgender girls find it difficult to have orgasms through penile stimulation. Anal stimulation is often a desirable option, especially if they are still attracted to women after transitioning.

14.2 THE EXPLOITATION REALITY

Unfortunately, these stories are fantasies, but the reality is often anything but a dream. In the book, a magic pill or magic device turns a cisgender man into a cisgender woman quickly, usually overnight or even in a few minutes. Reality is much different.

Page 129 of 219

14.2.1 FEMINIZATION REALITIES

The reality of feminization is that it can take up to 4 years to transition from living full-time as a male to living full-time as a female. And almost as long for transgender men to transition from female to male.

Even if a transgender girl transitions before puberty, they usually have to live part-time in the target gender for weekends and evenings during the prior year and live as a girl 24/7 during the summer before starting school as a girl.

Hiding out isn't an option. Transgender clients must meet with therapists and create a network of friends who will support them when they start school.

For the post-puberty, the realities of feminization can be long and painful. As mentioned before, there may include electrolysis, facial surgery, plucking, waxing, laser, blockers, hormones, breast implants, and bottom surgery. There's also the hours of practice and socialization skills required to not just pass but "blend" in with other women. The transgender girl is pretty enough to get positive feedback and yet not so pretty that people start staring and obsessing. They don't give oglers time to notice the things that might otherwise have gone unnoticed. Even the most aggressive timetable can be 2-8 years to fully transition. And this is assuming that everything has been planned out exceptionally well.

Often, a well-planned transition may include relocation. Changing jobs to an employer who is LGBT friendly. It can often involve painful steps like divorce, home loss, family, and child support.

14.2.2 NEGLECT AND REJECTION

For many transgender girls, even if a partner is supportive initially.
There may be a point where support turns to neglect. Romance turns
into roommates. The love turns into apathy and finally into rejection.
In some cases, the wife becomes the domestic abuser of her
transitioning "husband." She refuses to accept her as a "wife." She
may tear him down emotionally. She'll try to shake his confidence
by telling him he looks ridiculous or horrible. She may even know
that he is becoming suicidal.

Rejection by a loved one can often be more painful than rejection by
parents and siblings. The love, romance, hopes, and dreams of the
marriage and relationship often disintegrate into an abusive and
hostile relationship that can shatter the transgender girl's hope of
ever being loved.

14.2.3 BLACKMAIL & EXTORTION

Another considerable risk is that the partner will start using
blackmail and extortion. The wife may threaten to seize all assets
and take custody. She'll threaten to have visitation revoked and
demand the house. She'll demand the entire retirement account and
the house while he makes the payment. There's even a risk that the
spouse would demand complete control of the transgender girl's
company, assets, and patents.

15 Iron Mask

The few transgender kids who survive puberty and haven't started transition and survived to their mid-twenties. Many transgender people try to settle into routine life based on the expectations of others and try to make the best of it.

I call this phase the Iron Mask – this is when the visible side of the mask shows a smiling happy face that appears to be happy. On the inside of the mask are jagged edges that cut into the real face.

15.1 Assimilation

Assimilation looks like acceptance. The transgender person appears to have "grown out of it." Nothing could be further from the truth. Rather than covert suicide, there is apathy about life. They apply their skills and talents, but there is no joy in the win, no pleasure in success, the praise isn't even heard, and even the pay is not a great reward.

The transgender person is now a prisoner in their own body. They may have moments of pleasure, but they are always painfully aware of their chains. The transgender girl sees the woman in the pretty dress at work, the lovely dress at church, or even the cute dress in the club. They are painfully reminded that they are now prisoners who can never express who they really are. They must always wear the mask. They must always quietly carry their burden and stay in the dark corners.

Public recognition only increases the pain, so they avoid it. Becoming famous makes the idea of coming out and transitioning seem even more impossible. It makes their spouse/jailer even more likely to do more damage. It is better to work behind the scenes and put someone else on the podium, even if you're writing the speeches they read.

15.1.1 CYNICISM

The resignation often gives way to cynicism. Avoiding the home entirely, drinking, drugs, overeating, eating high fat, high salt, high carb diets, eating junk food out of the vending machines, drinking sugared soda, and just withdrawing from the world socially. Avoid personal conversations by dumping factoids to the point of being annoying enough that people stop inviting them to lunch, drinks after work, or any other social events.

15.1.2 EXISTENCE

Existence is but an illusion. This is about the point where someone looks forward to Mondays because they can't wait to get to work to avoid the pain of their personal life, especially their inability to transition. While working, they often get "In the zone", putting in 15-18 hours with only bathroom breaks. Even eating at their desks to take on more significant challenges.

What's missing too often is teamwork, listening to others, and bouncing ideas off each other.

15.1.3 KARMA & DHARMA

Part of what may be keeping them alive is the concept of Karma and Dharma. Karma requires that they live in a way that helps others in this life to do well in the next life. Dharma or destiny is the belief that they are put in this life to fulfill a purpose, and if they don't do it in this life, they will be required to achieve that purpose in the next life.

15.2 THE DEEP SECRET

Another dimension of life, especially for older transgender women, is their ability to keep secrets. Often, to survive through puberty without being killed, locked up, or killing themselves, they have learned to imitate the mannerisms of a cisgender person. The transgender girl can look and act enough like a cisgender man to avoid bullying, harassment, and discrimination at its worst. This doesn't mean that they have "Grown out of it". It just means they have become very good at hiding that they are still girls on the inside.

Transgender men are less overt but often become adept at "dressing for comfort." No matter how masculine they look, they assert that they are just women dressing comfortably. They may even get married and have children. Other transgender men will dress situation-appropriate, baggy cords for the daytime around the house, but skirt and heels for a night of clubbing. But for him, the skirt and heels are just a drag costume that helps them score with guys. The problem is that it may be hiding their true desire to be accepted as a man.

15.2.1 CROSS-DRESSING IN SECRET

Transgender girls often cross-dress in secret, but they are far more creative and adept at hiding their stash. When posing as cisgender men, the transgender girl might add secret compartments in the ceiling, walls, stairwells, built-ins, and so on.

Some transgender girls had been cross-dressing for 30 years of marriage before being discovered. Often, the discovery is such a betrayal that the wife loses all trust. The entire marriage goes sour. If her husband presented himself as a sexist alpha male who refused to do "women's work," this might be understandable.

Page 134 of 219

Even if he was never a sexist, never abusive, had an even temper, was nurturing and supportive. He helped with the kids, cooked meals, cleaned the kitchen, and was very generous in the bedroom. Yet the wife feels deceived, betrayed, and angry.

Sometimes she is angry because she wishes she had known earlier to enjoy this from the beginning. She might even help her husband transition, even if only on weekends. Other times they wish they had known so they could have avoided the marriage in the first place. This often destroys the marriage.

Unfortunately, the husband is often too ashamed and afraid to share with his wife. He can't share the bullying, torments, physical abuse, and worse he experienced long before meeting her. He can't express how he had hoped that the marriage would help him stop wanting to be a cross-dresser, let alone transgender. He may not even be able to share how he loved doing all those things many alpha men call "women's work" because he enjoyed doing it.

Even if the marriage survives, much of the intimacy is lost unless she can accept the transgender girl. Because if she doesn't, the transgender girl will withdraw from the wife.

15.2.2 FETISH DRESSING

Many cross-dressers will limit their activities to fetish dressing. Often just panties or some other single garment, and just for the period long enough to reach orgasm, then they can't get it off fast enough. A transgender girl, however, is more likely to wear more items. She may wear stockings, a corset or garter belt, panties, a bra, a slip, and even a little black dress. Often the wardrobe is selected to be stashed, meaning it won't need to be ironed, dry cleaned, or hung up in a closet.

The transgender girl generally doesn't rush to orgasm unless she really must. She may even try to avoid anything that would mess up the clothes. A condom or pad will help protect the clothing from an accidental spill. And when an orgasm is achieved, IF it is completed, there is no rush to get everything off, and she might even wait until the last possible moment.

15.2.3 BUSINESS TRIPS OR HOME ALONE

Transgender women often look for opportunities to dress for an extended period. The most common method is to go on business trips. They may spend the whole night in their hotel room at this phase, often dressing immediately after eating. She may even order room service to dress as soon as the food is delivered and stay dressed for the rest of the night. They may even remain dressed all night long, either in a nightie or in lingerie they like.

Another opportunity is to stay home alone while the rest of the family visits the wife's parents or goes on a vacation trip. This is an opportunity to spend an entire day or even a whole weekend dressed, cooking, and doing everything else like a girl. She may even clean the apartment or house because she wants the opportunity to have more of these home-alone experiences.

15.3 THE DUAL LIFE

The dual life is another version of the Iron Mask. In this case, their spouse may know that their partner likes to dress up, but they have avoided discussions of the actual transition. In this case, the spouse may be a willing participant, a reluctant participant, or a non-participant. The important thing is that there is awareness on the spouse's part.

15.3.1 DRESSING FOR SEX

If the spouse is willing, the early stages of a relationship may actually enjoy fulfilling each other's fantasies, including their husband's desire to dress up for sex. In fact, they may want to keep the dressing in the bedroom as a way to avoid having it expand to any form of public dressing.

If the husband is transgender and eager to please his wife like a girl, she may really enjoy the extra time, the more intense pleasure, and the lack of rush. The wife may even enjoy her willingness to learn, to take direction, and to explore the wife's deepest desires. If letting him dress up means unique and wonderful sexual experiences consistently, the wife may be pretty happy to continue to let her husband dress in private for years. So long as he doesn't want to take it out of the bedroom.

Of course, the wife will become aware of the girl inside, and the longer they are together, the more obvious she becomes. If the wife is bisexual, this may work out quite well. If she is heterosexual, she may find herself losing interest, losing respect, and losing love. Conversely, the husband may start losing his interest in women or may stop initiating or start initiating too much.

15.3.2 TEA PARTIES

In the cross-dressing community, a common practice is "tea parties." These are opportunities to get fully dressed as a woman and spend time with other cross-dressers. In some of these groups, transgender girls are welcome. In others, they are not.

15.3.3 PRIVATE CLUBS

In some cities, some private clubs or groups range from transgender support to the houses of the pageant community. Most of these are exclusive and often by invite only, or an invitation can be requested by answering many questions.

16 DOMESTIC ABUSE & NEGLECT

Unfortunately, when a spouse finds out that their spouse is transgender, it often does not go well. Suppose a heterosexual, cisgender spouse must face that their spouse is not the man/woman they appear to be. In that case, the spouse of a transgender person can become very abusive in so many ways.

16.1 GASLIGHTING – WIFE

When a wife becomes abusive, one of the first tactics is gaslighting. Every time her spouse is home, she becomes abusive, telling him everything she doesn't like about him. She often finds her own self-esteem suffering and wants to make her spouse feel even worse than he already does. She may or may not know about his prior abuse and being bullied. Still, even if she does, she can be ruthless, insulting him as a provider, as a housekeeper, as a parent, and as a lover. She tears down his already fragile self-esteem day after day.

Often, the defense eventually devolves into avoiding home as much as possible. He may take on extra projects at work or get involved in activities away from home. In the worst case, it may take the form of going out drinking. Other "escapes" can include golf, tennis, or even exercise class. Many who have trouble with drinking will go to 12 step meetings. Even when they are home, they stop listening to the abuse, which irritates the spouse.

To keep the husband vulnerable, she will often come on to him sexually and then mock him as soon as he shows interest. One woman said, "We have sex three times a year just so he'll remember what he is NOT getting." In effect, her goal was to emotionally castrate him. Castrating him to the point where he no longer wants her. But will continue to give her nearly all his money.

Keep in mind that the wife is trying to force the husband into gender conformity, which intensifies the Gender Dysphoria described above. The husband may be forced to wear suits and ties or sweatshirts and blue jeans. Gender Dysphoria just gets worse.

16.2 GASLIGHTING – HUSBAND

When a husband gaslights his wife, he often insults her looks. He calls her stupid. He treats her like a servant. He tells her she's ugly. He scolds her because she said things she didn't. He punishes her because she did something she didn't. He blames her for things that aren't her fault. The goal is to tear away self-esteem and security to create more dependency and control.

The wife may be forced to wear the skirts and tight blouses her husband wants to see. She faces verbal and emotional abuse if she wears pants or baggy tops or doesn't look "right" to her husband.

16.3 BLACKMAIL

Simple and subtle emotional abuse like gaslighting can quickly turn to something even darker. The spouse knows a secret and knows who shouldn't know. It might be a parent or grandparent, the employer, the people at church, or the school social worker. Of course, blackmail only works if you have the correct information, the suitable proof, and know who can't be told. If they get it wrong or the secret is leaked, the blackmailer loses all power.

16.4 VIOLENCE, RAPE, & CHASTITY

Perhaps the cruelest forms of abuse involve sexual abuse by spouses. The husband beats and rapes his wife because she got a short haircut. The wife ties her husband up in his sleep or on the promise of some "kinky sex" only to rape them with candles, broomsticks, or worse. Wives have even used chloroform or ether to knock out their sleeping husbands to ensure they don't wake up while being bound. There are no safe words, no "green, yellow, red." In fact, an abusive spouse often thrives on the terror and fear fueled by their hatred of their transgender spouse.

A recent development has been the male chastity cage. The testes hold this cage in place and then lock and cannot be removed. Often, a wife will use this cage on her husband and then mail the key to a friend or relative. This is to make sure that her husband knows that he will be unable to safely get out of the cage without submitting to all demands. Of course, even then, he may not be able to get out of the cage.

16.5 EXPLOITATION

Exploitation is the opposite of blackmail. In this case, the secret is told in the most public way possible. The wife may post pictures of him to social media accounts. The husband may post photos of his transgender spouse with his binder and his short haircut, letting the whole world know "she thinks she's a man." Sometimes they will even show her with bruised breasts.

In this case, the spouse wants to completely humiliate their transgender spouse and destroy their reputation, isolate them completely, sever all relationships and friendships, and even destroy their career. The damage can be extreme.

Page 140 of 219

16.6 FINANCIAL

Often, especially a spouse is considering ending the marriage. When the transgender spouse has access to funds or income, the cisgender spouse will look for ways to gain control of as many resources as possible. Buy a house and put the mortgage in his name and the title in her name. Get named as an equal holder of the 401K. Get control of the checkbooks and credit cards. Max out the credit cards and move cash from the joint account into personal accounts.

Often, the cisgender spouse will max out the credit cards. They'll buy furniture, electronic equipment, and other things they will need to set up their new house. They'll give the junk furniture to the transgender spouse. If they have a new boyfriend or girlfriend, they may buy them presents. In some cases, they will even purchase collectibles and other marketable items they can sell for cash later. There have even been cases where the cisgender spouse has applied for additional credit cards in her husband's name without his knowledge, then maxed those out as well.

16.7 ISOLATION

The cisgender spouse often tries to isolate their transgender spouse from all support groups, friends, family, and work friends. She may even force him to join a new church that is homophobic and transphobic. He may take her with his wife to meet his drinking buddies just to make sure she can't talk to other friends. The goal here is to isolate them and overwhelm them with negative messages from everyone they associate with.

16.8 INFIDELITY

Even if the cisgender spouse was faithful before, they might start to
cheat. They often reach such complete control that they will very
openly start having affairs. They'll even flaunt their new
relationships. The cisgender husband will flaunt his new partners
who wear miniskirts and heels. They'll look and dress like his
favorite fantasies and introduce them to his ugly hideous wife, who
thinks she's a man. The cisgender wife may find an alpha male.
She'll make it a point to let him meet her "sissy husband," who
could never be man enough and could never be a woman, even an
ugly one.

Ironically, the cisgender spouse not only understands gender
dysphoria but does everything they can to increase the amount of
gender dysphoria. In some cases, they may even hope that their
spouse will kill themselves so they can get the insurance money
before there is a divorce.

16.9 PARENTING

When a parent first sees their own child, it's a beautiful moment,
one of the most beautiful moments in their lives. The bonding of a
parent to their child is almost universal. Even in those first seconds,
there are possibilities. Then the doctor announces "boy" or "girl,"
and half the possibilities disappear in 5 seconds.

16.9.1 CHILDREN AS A HOPE

For a transgender parent, there is the hope of living vicariously through their children. The transgender man imagines being able to play catch with their son. The transgender woman imagines being able to play Barbies with their daughter. They dream of taking them clothes shopping as they get older. If anything, those transgender parents are better parents, even though still living in the cisgender iron mask. They are often a better parent because they genuinely want to be part of every stage of their children's lives. They don't want to judge or repress them the way they have been repressed.

Their time together is wonderful and memorable, especially if the other spouse is abusive. In some homes, the children may be the only comfort to a transgender spouse in the iron mask. In fact, the transgender parent may even prefer to "give mom a break" by taking the kids out somewhere to have fun away from the abusive cisgender parent. Kids aren't stupid, and they don't like seeing either parent being abused.

16.9.2 CHILDREN AS A WEAPON

Unfortunately, children also become a tool or weapon to hold the "girl inside" or "boy inside" in check to keep them hidden. Even more so with the transgender girl, the cisgender spouse can use fear of the kids finding out to avoid any dressing situations and prevent any consideration of the transgender person outing themselves.

Just to lock in the secrecy, the cisgender spouse may take the kids to a homophobic and transphobic church. The kids will get imbued with the message that homosexuals and transsexuals are sick disgusting perverts who should be killed. This way, by the time the kids do find out, the discovery will hopefully make them hate the transgender spouse.

16.9.3 *"Protecting" the Children*

Another reason for going to a homophobic and transphobic church is that it is an excellent place to meet allies who will help with the persecution of the transgender spouse. In the Sunday school class, one of the women can introduce them to a social worker member and another lawyer to help them initiate the divorce proceedings.

During or after the divorce proceedings, the cisgender wife can have the homophobic social worker write a letter advising the court that the husband's visitation is "detrimental to the children's welfare." She can recommend that visitation be revoked entirely or limited to 1 hour of supervised visitation every month. By waiting until after the divorce, the husband has committed himself to generous child support and alimony commitment on the expectation of an amicable divorce. Only to find out that the plot was to steal the children and the money.

17 STABILITY

The fantastic illusion for a transgender person is that of apparent stability. It is often hiding the storm of Gender Dysphoria underneath. Some transgender women transition when they are 65 and retired to transition without losing their income. Yet they tell stories of the pain they struggled with as they waited all those years.

17.1 THE VELVET TRAP

The velvet trap is when life starts to become successful. College is completed, and they are successful at their career. Their family or living situation is stable, and they have friends and even lead social groups. But they also have hidden Gender Dysphoria.

17.1.1 CAREER

In their career, hard work, imagination, and the ability to deliver results in promotions, leadership positions, and recognition. But the trap is that they must "butch up," and the more they cooperate, the more they must conform, the more recognition they get. But the trap is that they can't be authentic. They can't even risk being out in any community.

17.1.2 DOMESTIC

By "playing the role," keeping everything a secret, and not even dressing, a transgender girl can be a pretty good husband and provider. A transgender boy can become a recognized and established professional and even an executive. However, the higher they rise, the more impossible it becomes to even consider the possibility of transition. Gender Dysphoria screams every night but must be silenced on the commute to work.

17.1.3 S*ocial Success*

With professional success comes social success. The golf clubs, the charity events, the political fundraisers, the embrace of the church. People want to make contact, some wanting a handout, others wanting to help in some way.

But again, with this recognition, the prospect of transition becomes more impossible, and Gender Dysphoria gets even worse.

17.1.4 T*he Dark Side*

The more Gender Dysphoria is repressed, the more the girl inside or the boy inside becomes the enemy. As one therapist put it, "If you try to kill the girl, the girl will kill you." The velvet trap may seem like a comfortable chair, but it's really the velvet rope used to form the noose. The self-destruction may be more overt but no less deadly.

18 COVERT SUICIDE

Often, older transgender people seem to have a happy and successful life. Still, the reality for so many older transgender people is that they are miserable on the inside and switch from overt suicide attempts and sudden death accidents to more covert methods. Essentially, this is "Suicide on the Installment Plan," with the final balloon payment that seals the deal.

18.1 ALCOHOLISM

The most accessible and most socially acceptable form of covert suicide is alcoholism. Drinking too much, too often, driving on dark, deserted roads around midnight, and taking long walks. Sometimes the drinking establishments are chosen for their danger. Drinking at a leather bar, a biker bar, a cowboy bar, or in bars located in rough neighborhoods. Drinking at places known for frequent fights and brawls, and even places where the violence turns to deadly weapons are popular places for transgender people. Transgender guys often start fights they may be able to win, but just as they start winning, they are confronted by a gang of violent thugs. Transgender girls may wear the boys' clothes, but they know which buttons to press to send one or more guys into a rage through verbal insults and innuendo. If someone gets cited for DUI or Drunk and Disorderly more than a few times, there is a good chance they are looking to the end game.

18.2 DRUG ADDICTION

Drug addiction is another popular way to get into the whole suicide on the installment plan for a shorter period.

18.2.1 PRESCRIPTION AND OTC

Transgender people caught in the velvet trap very often turn to prescription drugs. Drugs to help them sleep, medications to help their blood pressure, pills to treat a variety of mental health and physical health problems. Going to lots of different doctors who don't know about each other. Getting prescriptions for depression, heart problems, and other health problems enables the legal junkie to get combinations that can be stronger than heroin, even opioids. Add OTC drugs like antihistamines, stimulants, and sedatives. Mixing a bunch of them up together can create life-threatening "accidental" drug interactions.

They may even use drugs to manage their medications, for example, taking Benadryl while drinking Scotch at night and taking Tedral and extra strong coffee in the morning.

18.2.2 RECREATIONAL DRUGS

Often, the successful transgender person has the money for elite drugs. Powder cocaine, GHB, Ecstasy, and other high-intensity drugs. Drugs that often don't show up on drug tests. Drugs that don't show up on breath tests. Drugs with low-grade misdemeanor charges, probation, and sometimes even aren't illegal because the compounds can't be identified. Drugs made of styrene or low-grade toxins. Remember that LSD was microscopic amounts of the byproducts of ergot fungus that grew in rye plants. Similar toxic compounds are sold in recreational doses.

18.3 OBESITY

This one sounds funny, "suicide by Big Mac." Essentially, eating high carb, high fat, low fiber diets three or more meals a day, eating candy from the vending machine, or bringing a backpack full of candy and sugared soft drinks.

Doing this daily for only a few years can trigger obesity. Weight gains of a hundred pounds or more over a short period are common. Often, the gain is so fast that people develop type 2 diabetes and progress directly on to kidney failure, liver failure, and heart failure.

18.4 HYPERTENSION

Adding a lot of fat and salt to the diet above, like potato chips and lots of salt on the steak and potatoes, can compound obesity. With high blood pressure and edema, water builds up, causing swelling in the ankles, feet, legs, arms, lungs, and heart. When combined with drugs and alcohol, heart attacks and strokes often hit as young as 45.

18.5 SMOKING

Smoking is less common today than before, but smoking and vaping are very effective ways to introduce large quantities of poison over a short period. The average smoker's life span is about 30 pack-years for an average person. Essentially, suppose a smoker smokes one pack of regular-length cigarettes every day for 30 years. In that case, they will die of lung disease or other cardiovascular diseases. If that same smoker smokes 3 packs of longs and covers the perforations to get the full "kick," they could be facing their first life-threatening conditions in less than 8-10 years. Because vaping is a purer form of nicotine, it can be even more deadly over an even shorter time.

Bans on smoking in the workplace, restaurants, bars and other public spaces have resulted in far fewer deaths due to these causes. Still, many smokers didn't live long enough to collect social security because they were chain smokers.

18.6 HEART DISEASE

We've already talked about the eating and salt habits that can lead to heart disease. Add lack of exercise, burning the candle on both ends for a couple of decades. The result can be life-threatening heart conditions that are difficult to detect, unexpected, and often ignored by the patient. The long days and short nights can lead to heart arrhythmias. The most common end for them is being found in the morning, in the office, hunched over a computer. Often, they don't even know they are dying. They may just think they are falling asleep.

Cardiovascular disease has more symptoms, but for someone on the "suicide installment plan," these symptoms are often ignored. The pain in the left arm is ignored, dismissed as RSI, or just muscle aches. Even when the pains shoot from wrist to neck, someone on the installment plan will prop themselves up. They'll take some pain killers, avoid being noticed and avoid getting treatment.

I have seen many of those on the "installment plan" refuse to let anyone touch them and refuse treatment even as they are losing consciousness. Some people even have medic-alert bracelets with DNC (Do Not Core) indicators. A message to paramedics and ambulance workers to NOT attempt to defibrillate them or administer CPR. Not all of them are transgender, but it's nearly hard to tell.

18.7 STROKE

Stroke often comes with little or no warning, and often there isn't enough warning to prevent severe damage or death. For others, there are warning signs. TIAs are transient attacks where the blockage may be temporary or the warning signs of blocked or bursting minor blood vessels.

For someone on the installment plan, the response to these warning signs is to dismiss it as a headache, even aggravating the situation with stimulants, Tylenol, or salt to worsen the situation. So often, their fear is that someone might try to save them and turn them into invalids, unable to speak or communicate. As a result, they may even deliberately try to isolate themselves, to prevent discovering their body until it's too late.

18.8 ACCIDENTS

Accidents are the most common form of death for adults under 60. Traffic accidents, falls, accidental drug overdose, accidental poisoning, and even just slip and fall in the tub. Do some indoor gardening and spray some weed killer or insecticide that is "accidentally" inhaled or ends up in the iced tea. So many accidents are not accidents. Police don't have the budget to investigate accidents.

18.9 STDs, AIDS

This is often a problem for younger transgender kids or transgender adults who are straying covertly. Many STDs can be caught and transmitted, but for someone on the "installment plan", not investigating or reporting it is an effective end-game strategy. Instead of taking the drugs that can save their lives, they avoid detection, then avoid the diagnosis, and keep forgetting to take medications or renew prescriptions.

18.10 OTHER EXIT RAMPS

Less obvious exit ramps include not taking necessary treatments or taking too much. Carrying over 8,000mg per day of Tylenol can cause liver damage. Antihistamines can cause dehydration and heart rhythm problems. And knowing you have cancer or diabetes gives someone on the installment plan a timeline to hope for.

In summary, those with gender dysphoria can find 1001 ways to die, and most of the time, even their loved ones won't realize that they wanted to die.

19 TRANSITION

The ONLY Effective Treatment for Acute Gender Dysphoria is transition. Treatments may delay the negative outcome, and transition does not guarantee a positive result. Still, overall, the prognosis is far better for those who transition.

The regret rate for transition is less than 1%. About 5% may detransition. Most of those who detransition do it due to external pressures. A transgender woman may detransition to protect her children from an abusive mother or stepfather. A transgender man may detransition to be with a loved dying relative. A transgender child may detransition due to bullying or family pressures not shared with therapists.

Detransition doesn't even reset the time bomb. Still, it may stop the timer long enough to deal with the crisis, but it starts ticking again once it is averted.

One of the popular myths is that it is possible to use various forms of "Conversion Therapy" to "brainwash" someone out of their gender dysphoria or sexual preference. They often claim success based on a handful of success stories. Usually, bisexual men who were given a choice between homosexual rape and abuse or a willing and sexually aggressive female partner "served on a silver platter." Conversion is only 5% effective with transgender clients.

Unfortunately, most of these programs are not monitored supervised by court officers. They have never been subjected to FDA field trials. Part of the reason is that so many of these programs still resort to torture, rape, verbal abuse, physical abuse, sleep deprivation, and even shock therapy. All these treatments have been outlawed, but conversion therapy programs are generally conducted under the shield of "religious counseling" and claim to be protected by the First Amendment. In addition, both the parents and the person getting the "conversion therapy" must sign waivers of liability and consent saying they are consenting as "members of the church."

Unfortunately, "conversion therapy" is a big dollar industry that preys on parents trying to force their kids to be "normal". Parents often pay more for "conversion therapy" than HRT, GCS, and breast enlargement or removal combined. Then they have funeral and graveyard costs.

When conversion therapy was practiced by medical practitioners, most frequently psychologists and psychiatric hospitals, the result that WAS monitored was abysmal. 90% of those subjected to medically supervised "conversion therapy" ended up killing themselves within a year of treatment.

Even "Gentle Aversion", having an MSW or LCSW try to discourage the client from transitioning is dangerous. They often focus on all the negatives and adverse consequences that might happen and reinforce and validate those fears, with no offer of hope beyond the losses. Even for this more covert form of aversion therapy, the suicide rates were unusually high. Most didn't live past their 25th birthday.

Police wouldn't investigate suicides or accidents unless they are alerted to a murder element such as bullying, cyberbullying, blackmail, threats, recent trauma, or apparent signs of rape. Even this is often limited to the coroner's autopsy report and is rarely investigated by SVU.

19.1 CHILDHOOD TRANSITION

So, let's talk about the process of transition. Many people, especially transphobes, love to paint the picture of the alpha male coming to school in an ill-fitting dress. Saying, "Hey coach, I'm a girl, and I want to shower with the girls," and being allowed to do so. Mike Huckabee was one of the most famous proponents of this myth.

The other popular myth is that parents can go to a doctor, start their 8-year-old boy on blockers and estrogen, and get the boy parts "cut off" the following week. This is probably the most flagrant display of total ignorance and misinformation circulating these days. In England, transphobic lawmakers used this argument to ban ALL transition-oriented therapy for transgender children.

19.1.1 IDENTITY ACCEPTANCE

By the time they are four or five years old, most kids know they are girls or boys. Boys want to play with other boys, girls want to play with other girls. Transgender kids are NO DIFFERENT. A transgender girl sees herself as a girl. She may cry and even scream during haircuts and complain about her scratchy boy clothes. A transgender boy will tear up dresses and roll up her big brother's blue jeans six inches to wear boy's clothes and wear his flannel shirts with the sleeves rolled up a few inches to fit the brother's boy shirts. If they must wear boy clothes, they will try to pick shorts and pink or purple soft T-shirts.

Yet even the simple acts of giving the transgender girl a haircut, or buying the transgender boy a dress, sends a message. It tells the child that they are not accepted. They are not loved, and they are not real people. It tells them that they must pretend to be boys or girls, even though they hate it. If the hostility is intense enough, the transgender child will go undercover immediately and repress even his memory, but not the pain of rejection.

So, of course, the very first part of any transition therapy is simply the acceptance of a transgender child's true identity. The doctor took 10 seconds to ASSIGN a gender, based on what he saw between the baby's legs. The child has confirmed their identity after 4-5 years of research. Almost from the time they could walk, they gravitated toward others of their own kind. Transgender girls gravitated toward girls, and transgender boys gravitated toward the other boys. Transgender boys gravitated toward the other boys. By the time they are 4-5 years old, a cisgender boy would resist wearing a dress, and a cisgender girl would resist getting a haircut.

It is essential to understand that the child's TRUE gender is the one they claim to be at 4-5 years old. The one they got as a baby was the ASSIGNED Gender. Accepting the child's TRUE Gender is the same as accepting a cisgender child's gender. If the child says they are a girl, don't cut her hair, let her buy girl shorts and girl tops, let her have dolls and unicorns. If the child says they are a boy, ask if he wants a haircut, let him tell the barber how short to cut it, and buy him new denim jeans and new flannel shirts in his size.

There are NO drugs, no surgeries, and no permanent changes at this stage. Furthermore, there is no reason anyone needs to know what's between their legs. Yes, the transgender boy will need to use a stall even to pee. The transgender girl will also use the stall and always sit to pee. These children deserve privacy the same way cisgender children deserve privacy. Genitalia should not be a "show and tell" exercise for cisgender or transgender kids. School rules should reinforce state and local laws against peeping, flashing, groping, and assault in bathrooms.

At this young age, a transgender child usually sees a therapist about once a month, first for initial diagnosis and confirmation of the child's IDENTITY. The therapist will ask about friends and family relationships with parents and siblings. They may even ask about extended family. The initial sessions will assess where the child is in expressing their identity.

19.1.2 SOCIALIZATION SKILLS

One of the things the therapist will do is help the child build confidence in socialization skills. Children who transition before 1st grade are often already thoroughly socialized. Transgender kids who transition during summer vacation or after a move can also establish a social network of others of their true gender. The transgender girl will have lots of girls as friends, a transgender boy will have lots of boys as friends.

For kids who transition later, there may be a period of living as their TRUE GENDER. Evenings and weekends during the school year. Then they transition to their TRUE GENDER full-time during the summer and make as many friends as possible during these transition periods. Even if people remember their previous gender, this network of friends will provide protection and support and issue a clear message. "She's one of us!" or "He's one of us!"

Fighting or wrestling among boys is normal, and a transgender boy may have to fight to earn his place in the pecking order. Still, they are more likely to be fair fights that end when one of the boys says, "I give," or "I yield!" or "You win!" to end the fight. At the end of the fight, the two will end up friends. At minimum, they will respect each other.

Of course, there will always be bullies and mean kids. However, when a bully realizes that the transgender kid does not stand alone, they are more reluctant to pick on that kid as a victim.

Page 157 of 219

The more significant threat is parents who find out and get homophobic or transphobic. They may encourage their children to attack as a gang. A preacher may call on several schoolmates to bully the transgender kid as a group. And he may even tell them where, when, and how so that they can do it without getting caught and so that they can make sure there are no "innocent witnesses" who can speak out against them. Ironically, transgender kids who haven't transitioned are more likely to be bullied by these groups. When they are forced to live as their assigned gender, they don't fit.

19.1.3 INTEGRATION

As the child begins living as their True Gender, they will generally integrate into their school culture. The boys will pick on transgender girls the way they pick on any other girl. The transgender boys will rough house with the cisgender boys the same way they would rough house with any other boy.

19.1.4 GROUND RULES

Of course, transgender kids also need to understand some strict ground rules. The "No peeping, flashing, groping, threats, or grabbing" rules are strict, they are laws, and these laws cut both ways. The girl who pries open the door of a transgender girl and tries to snap a picture of her body parts is the one committing the crime. If she publishes it on social media, she is committing a felony. If she tries to incite violence with the picture, she could even be guilty of a hate crime.

The most important thing for transgender kids to know is to be honest, and trust teachers, authorities, parents, and therapists. If their privacy is invaded, it should be reported to parents immediately, as well as teachers.

19.2 TEEN TRANSITION

Teen transition adds to the complication of puberty. Ideally, the child will be able to transition BEFORE Puberty. Transgender kids learn about puberty and get very freaked out. A voice crack might just be a dry throat, but to a transgender girl, it's a nightmarish warning that their voice could change at any time. They will be checking for hair growth and for Adam's apple. Transgender boys will be freaking out at even the slightest tenderness in their breasts.

19.2.1 BLOCKERS

Doctors try to start blockers as late and as little as possible. They use blood tests to see the jump in hormones. Then they introduce the blockers using the lowest possible dose. They run blood tests. If necessary, they increase the dosage to suppress the unwanted hormones to pre-puberty levels. Usually, they will do it over a few months, using the blockers only. When the child has met the prerequisites for hormones, including age, experience, socialization, and visibility, hormones will be added to the blockers.

The child may decide to stop the hormones and be cisgender and experience normal puberty at any point in this process. For most transgender kids, stopping isn't even an option, and they are chomping at the bit to start their hormones. Typically, the wait is two to four years.

19.2.2 HORMONES

If the child has shown all the socialization, networking, and integration skills described in the section for transgender kids before puberty, they become candidates for hormones. The doctor will have several considerations. They don't want to start them so soon that it stunts the child's growth, but they want to start in time to share the experience of breast growth with the other girls. In the United States, doctors often begin low-dose hormones at around 14 years old, usually as pills. The doctor then checks hormone levels to see where the child is relative to their True Gender.

The doctor will also be looking carefully for any signs of hormone levels that are too HIGH. They don't want patients to take too much, take "herbal supplements," or use black-market hormones. Any of these can be time for a serious discussion. Some transgender kids want to rush things along by doing something to increase their dosages to "make my boobs come quicker and bigger" or "make my beard come in faster and sing bass." Usually, the kids are cautious unless a doctor is TOO conservative. The test results are visible to the patient and their parents. It is straightforward for transgender kids to see that they are around the norms for their target gender. It's vital for the doctor to understand what's required to treat a transgender patient. If the hormone levels are too low, the breasts won't grow properly, or the voice won't change properly, and kids stop trusting their doctors.

HRT is usually required for life. Stopping or reducing estrogen levels can result in osteoporosis, dementia, and other conditions resulting from loss of both testosterone and estrogen.

19.2.3 TOP SURGERY

Usually, the minimum age for any surgical modification is 18. Top surgery may be available at age 15 with parental approval. Bottom surgery is not available to minors. Therefore it is so important to prevent breast growth in transgender boys.

Page 160 of 219

19.3 POST-PUBERTY TRANSITION

Starting transition after puberty complicates everything. Transgender people often refer to cisgender puberty as "Puberty Damage," and repairing that damage can be extremely painful, expensive, and sometimes disappointing.

19.3.1 TRANSGENDER GIRL

When a transgender girl goes through male puberty, there are many unwanted changes. Each of these can be corrected as described below.

19.3.1.1 Facial Electrolysis

The beard is the most apparent most male puberty change to correct. Even with thick maximum-coverage makeup, a dark beard can be tough to cover. I used to use theatrical stage makeup with theatrical concealer. Even if the shadow is covered immediately after a shave, the giveaway shadow can appear within hours of shaving. Shaving several times a day to live full-time is simply not an option.

For many therapists and doctors, removing this dark facial hair is one of the first milestones to be met for the post-puberty transition. The first problem is that the roots of male facial hair are much deeper and thicker and have a long wax-like root as well. To wax off a beard, it is necessary to grow it out to about 2 inches, then it needs to be waxed off using honey wax or hot wax. Pulling out thousands of these large course hairs is extremely painful and bloody. There is also the risk of facial scarring.

After all that pain, there will still be lots of hair that will grow back thinner, and other hair that will grow back as thick beard hair because it wasn't pulled out by the root. The second choice is laser or high-intensity light. These are great if you have dark hair and light skin. Numbing the face for flashing is often done using cold packs or ice in a baggy. 30 seconds of icing can keep the area numb for about 90 seconds. While one side is being zapped, the other side can be numbing. Then switch sides.

Even after flashing all that dark hair off, there is often a lot of thick white hair that will need to be removed some other way.

The only fully effective long-term removal technique is electrolysis. This process involves inserting a stylus into a hair follicle then hitting it with a weak electronic current. Each time there is moderate pain, all the hair treated must be removed by plucking or waxing. This is a time-consuming process, and the whole face can take four to eight hours. Many operators offer anesthesia for four-hour sessions. Usually, a minimum of five sessions per year are required to address each growth cycle.

19.3.1.2 Tracheal Shave

The next big issue is Adam's Apple. The bobbing nodule can be an obvious giveaway to expose even the most expertly feminized woman. This expensive surgery requires anesthesia and takes about a week of healing. Some people train themselves to keep it high on their neck. Others gain weight in their neck to hide it in their double chin. Not an ideal solution.

19.3.1.3 Facial Feminization Surgery

After puberty, masculine bone growth characteristics can be a real problem for transgender girls. A jaw that is too big, a brow that protrudes, a chin that is chiseled or too bulbous. Low cheekbones. Facial feminization surgery can be as expensive as gender confirmation (bottom) surgery. Surgeons recommend waiting until after 2 years of HRT. The hormones will redistribute fat and muscle tissue to create a more feminine look.

19.3.1.4 Vocal Training

Vocal training is a challenge of a different kind. A big giveaway that can be a big problem for transgender women is their voice. I've known several beautiful transgender women who are indistinguishable from cisgender women. Until they speak. Their baritone voice with chest resonance can make them stand out to anyone who hears them. This can even be dangerous when a young man who is not terribly bright is lusting for what he thinks is a beautiful woman. Then her voice is so obviously masculine that he freaks out. He can go homophobic, thinking that his attraction to this beautiful woman means he's gay.

There are several vocal training programs and vocal training apps that transgender women can use to help improve their voices. I like to think of babies or puppies, which puts my mind and voice in the right mood to speak like a girl and pass. Some coaches are great. Others are terrible.

Even good voice training often takes a post-puberty transgender woman a long time to develop a good voice. A voice that isn't too sexy or too high and is nasal enough to sound feminine.

Even then, it takes a lot of work and concentration. I used to have my "Debbie Voice" and my "Techie Voice" when I would describe technical issues. My voice would drop because I needed to concentrate on the complex issues and couldn't focus on my voice.

19.3.1.5 Vocal Surgery

There are surgeries to shorten or "band" the vocal cords. The voice can be raised quite a bit, but initially, after the surgery, the patient may feel like they sound like Minnie Mouse. It takes about a month to get used to the new voice and modulate it correctly. Other skills like singing can take months or years to remaster.

19.3.1.6 Waxing/Plucking Body Hair

For the same reason that male facial hair is difficult to remove, removing male body hair is problematic. Again, the most effective methods are waxing and plucking to pull the hair out by the deep roots. This can be extremely painful the first few times because the hair is so thick, and the roots are so deep. The waxing process needs to be done about 5 times during the first year with no shaving between each waxing. This can be followed up by epilator devices that can pluck the thinner hair with thinner roots that are sparser. It's less painful than using it on the original hair, and eventually, the hair is completely removed from the body.

19.3.1.7 Laser – Body Hair

Laser or high-intensity light such as iLight treatments are often an excellent alternative to waxing for places where you don't want to be shiny smooth. A woman has light and thin arm hair, but the hair needs to be there, or it becomes an obvious tell. The light treatments kill the darker hair and leave the lighter hair, which is also thinner. The look is more natural.

19.3.1.8 Genital Electrolysis

Before Gender Confirmation Surgery, most doctors now require genital electrolysis. The painful process performed on the face also must be done on the genitals. This is so painful that a more potent sedative is used as well as local anesthesia. These sessions usually take 4 hours each, and 5 sessions are needed to get the necessary level of hair removed.

19.3.1.9 BMI Requirements

Another requirement before GCS is performed is a BMI of 28 or lower. This is a requirement because a higher BMI increases the risks of complications during surgery and healing after. This surgery takes four to six hours to complete when everything is going well and can take twice as long when there are complications.

19.3.1.10   Insurance Issues

Most insurance companies will cover blockers and HRT because they are considered medically necessary by the AMA. Still, the therapist is mental health care and is often not as well covered, with copays as much as $25 per session. Most of the time, an LCSW is enough to meet the needs for coaching during Real Life Experience. Still, it is necessary to get a psychologist's approval for HRT and GCS. However, the psychologist usually defers to the judgment of the LCSW or MSW. The drugs themselves are remarkably inexpensive. Even at retail, the cost is less than $100/month for blockers and hormones.

Getting the surgery paid for can be tricky. Some employers make this coverage mandatory. Other companies do not cover breast augmentation or Gender Confirmation Surgery, also known as "Bottom Surgery," because it's not a visible necessity. Most insurance companies will cover an orchiectomy, also known as castration. This simple procedure can be done with local or regular anesthesia. The procedure takes about 20 minutes of actual surgery time.

19.3.1.11   Bottom Surgery

Gender Confirmation Surgery is three surgeries that may be done in the same surgical session or up to three separate surgeries. The first one is orchiectomy, removing the testes while leaving the scrotum, used later.

Page 165 of 219

The second is vaginoplasty. Contrary to popular myth, the penis is not removed but "inverted." The head of the penis and the nerve bundle to it are separated and turned into a sensitive clitoris. This is delicate microsurgery and was only perfected in the 1990s. The penis shaft is emptied of fibroid tissue that provides the bulk and veins that cause erections. The emptied penis is then turned inside-out to become the wall of the vagina. This new vagina must be positioned carefully so that the opening is in the same spot as a cisgender woman. If the penis is too small because the patient has been on blockers too long, extra depth can be provided using part of the sigmoid colon or skin grafts from the thigh or stomach.

The third surgery is labiaplasty. This procedure turns the scrotum into major and minor labia. Without the labiaplasty, the vagina looks unnatural. Most of the best surgeons will perform all three operations simultaneously. More cautious doctors, or when the procedure is more complicated involving grafts, will perform the labiaplasty separately.

Many transgender girls get the orchiectomy first to ensure they don't revert if they can't take the blockers. It's often the first significant step. Many will opt for the orchiectomy only.

Many opt for a zero-depth vaginoplasty. It includes the orchiectomy, creating a clitoris, and labiaplasty. The main advantage is that dilation is not required, and risks are much lower. This is popular among transgender lesbians.

19.3.1.12   Dilation

After the surgery, the new vagina must be dilated. Initially, this must be done several times a day and is very painful. Later, it only must be done once a day. Failure to dilate can result in a collapse or shrinking of the vagina. Over time the dilation becomes less painful and eventually becomes pleasurable.

After several months of dilation, it is possible to start having intercourse as a woman. Dilation and/or sexual intercourse will be required regularly for the rest of the transgender woman's life.

19.3.2 TRANSGENDER BOY

I don't have the personal experience of being a transgender boy. Still, I have known a few dozen over the years who have shared their experience of transition, both in-person and online. My apologies if I miss anything important.

19.3.2.1 Binding

For an adult transgender man, the early stages of transition and real-life experience require some form of binding of the breasts. Younger men, after puberty, often use cloth, ace bandages, or tape to bind the breasts. These more primitive methods can be hazardous because the tight binding of larger breasts can cut off circulation to the breasts. Causing fibroids, bruising, and even death of tissue that can become life-threatening.

A safer but often less effective option is the compression shirt. This shirt looks like a men's T-Shirt but has heavy elastic around the upper chest. Compression shirts are marginally safer because it provides uniform pressure throughout the breast area. Some transgender men have even had to wear two of these compression shirts to get enough compression. Fortunately, men's shirts are usually pretty baggy, so flannel or button-down dress shirts can hide anything the compression shirt can't.

19.3.2.2 Testosterone

The hormone therapy for a transgender man is testosterone. It takes remarkably little testosterone to shut down estrogen production and to produce male puberty. Within a few months, the voice begins to drop, the face starts growing a beard, and the weight distribution becomes more masculine. Their face will become masculine appropriate to their weight. Of course, most transgender men will also experience a period of acne as part of male puberty. After about 2 years of testosterone, there is no way to tell he was assigned female at birth.

19.3.2.3 Mastectomy

For a transgender man, mastectomy is often the first surgical procedure they want to be performed. This is the reverse of breast enlargement and is generally performed similarly. Incisions under the breasts and removal of the breast tissue. Removal of excess skin and pulling the remaining skin tight. Then putting in enough stitches that scars will be minimal. If necessary, nipple size is reduced as well. If he stays out of the sun for a year, he can take off his shirt and look like an average guy. He can get a tan the following year.

19.3.2.4 Bodybuilding

Part of the male body fat distribution is shifting weight to the belly. Many transgender men will prevent this with exercise and bodybuilding. Specifically, they will use the body-building techniques bodybuilders use to add bulk muscle. Lifting heavy weights causes tearing of the muscles, then giving them a day or two to repair the microtears builds bulk. In a matter of months, the combination of weightlifting, diet, and other exercises can produce a very handsome and desirable man.

19.3.2.5 Hysterectomy & Oophorectomy

Testosterone and blockers, if started early enough, can stop periods. Still, for those who transition a few years after puberty, the periods may continue for some time. Most transgender men don't feel an urgent need to have their ovaries or uterus removed. It's not visible, and they can successfully blend in with other men. If he does have the procedure done, the surgeon can also create the appearance of a scrotum. It's less complex than vaginoplasty but more complex than vasectomy.

19.3.3 PHALLOPLASTY

If a transgender man wants a penis, there are two options. The more modern approach uses topical testosterone on the clitoris and labia. This will cause the clitoris to grow even more than it does with the injected testosterone and can create a modest-sized "penis" with some of the wonderful sensations of one.

The other option is to create a penis from a skin graft configured as permanently erect. The upside is a realistic-looking penis with length and a permanent "hard-on," but the downside is the lack of sensation. There isn't an easy way to create the nerves and sensations of a male penis with a graft.

This lack of sensation may be one of the reasons why more transgender men are opting for topical testosterone. The results can be quite satisfactory if they start the topical testosterone and the injected testosterone early enough.

19.4 ADULT TRANSITION

Transitioning later in life can be much more complicated than transitioning as a child or teenager. More considerations, consequences, and complications can create challenges and limitations.

Congratulations, before transition, the transgender person has established themselves in a career, had several successful projects, gotten a few promotions, and became a visible leader in their profession. But then comes transition. What are the impacts?

19.4.1.1 Social Issues

One of the first significant challenges, especially for transgender women, is that the rules of the game change. As a man, the first part of a business meeting is a "pissing contest". Each of the men tries to "mark their territory." Establishing their area of expertise and rank within the group. In a more primitive culture, there might have been some punching and kicking involved. Still, in modern business meetings, the contests are more intellectual. Each man tries to establish the value and importance of their expertise and perspective the problem at hand.

The problem for a woman is that she should NOT participate in this process at all. She needs to listen carefully but NOT take "minutes" or "notes" for the group. Any notes she might be taking are for her personal use later. Only AFTER the men have finished their ranking and have gotten into an argument should the woman come in as "Momma" and "Clean up the mess." Having listened quietly, she can now ask questions, get details, and get the men to cooperate more closely with each other.

For a transgender man, the opposite is true. As a woman, she had learned to be the passive observer until it was time to "make the kill!" But as a man, he must be ready to establish his rank within the group, or his opinions won't be respected at all. Even if he ranks at the bottom, putting up a good "fight" will earn him the respect of his fellows.

One of the big mistakes a transgender woman may make early on is to accept the role of "secretary" or "note-taker" or "recorder" without also taking control of the meeting. It is important early on for a woman to \avoid this trap. They need to remind the good gentlemen that if they want her to play secretary during business hours, her billing rate is high, and her experience is deep. It would be a waste of time and effort to deal with the distractions of taking minutes. She can propose that the most junior team member take the notes, which she can review later and correct if necessary. The alternative is to take the notes but make sure that the notes reflect her position and concerns, so she becomes the key perspective in the meeting. This propaganda play will often result in an appreciation of her talents and the need to have a more impartial recorder.

19.4.1.2 Establishing Credentials

The medical transition process is challenging, but the legal process can be even more so. In the United States, changing your gender on your birth certificate can be trivial or downright impossible depending on the laws of the state you were born in. Some states only allow a birth certificate to be "amended," essentially stating when you started living as the new gender.

The first step is a legal name change, which in the United States requires a petition to the court, which can be done as a form, or a lawyer can file the petition. Many states require that a legal notice be posted in a local newspaper's personal column. So that creditors and law enforcement authorities know your previous and new name. It can get ugly to be exposed in this way, but this is usually quite rare. Lawyers and bean counters read legal notices, but not many others.

Page 171 of 219

There is a form that a doctor can fill out that can make it possible to change your gender on your driver's license. The certified copy of the court order allows you to change the name on the license. Then you can change the gender on your social security card and apply for a corrected passport.

This will provide the legal documents necessary to be employed and work legally under your new name and gender.

19.4.1.3 History Carry-over

A more significant challenge is keeping your previous history linked to your new name. Credit reporting agencies, banks, and other financial institutions must be notified. Many will need a photocopy of your court order and your new license with the new gender. Then they can change your history and accounts so that your good credit and sound financial records stay with you. Don't forget 401K and IRA accounts with current and previous employers.

It is illegal to try and use a name change or gender change to try and break the links in your history. For example, suppose you have prior criminal convictions or a poor credit rating. In that case, you can't use the new name to claim a recent credit history and a clean criminal record.

By the way, it is always best, to be honest about your history, including when you transitioned. If an employer is hostile to transgender people, you don't want to work there anyway. You would be fired as soon as they discovered the deception. On the other hand, many employers WANT transgender gender people working for them. Many of these companies pride themselves on their Diversity Programs. They don't tolerate bigotry because many of their most valuable resources are people of color and LGBTQ workers.

19.4.1.4 Overt/Covert discrimination

Discrimination and transphobia are sometimes overt and quite open.
The Transgender Exclusive Radical Feminist (TERF). The Religious
Liberty guy who hates queers while eating cheeseburgers. The guy
who watches Fox News every night because the female
commentators have nice legs.

The best weapon with these people is honesty. Do your best to
answer all their questions to the best of your ability. Even offer a bit
too much information when it's appropriate. For example, if a TERF
asks, "do you still have a penis," smile and hold your fingers a half-
inch apart and say "A teeny tiny one" apologetically. She will
become your new ally.

I have a lot of fun with the religious types. There are many excellent
articles on this. Most Christian Homophobia is based on only 10 to
15 verses out of over 30,000 verses in the Bible. There are only 8
verses that address homosexuality. The one in Leviticus 18
addresses FORCED homosexuality. A father giving his youngest
son as a "payment" in the form of a eunuch concubine. Giving a son
instead of a daughter. Usually, daughters were forced to marry
someone they didn't know. She was payment for the grazing or
water rights.

The one in Deuteronomy addresses homosexual rape. It's worth
noting that when a woman was raped, Deuteronomy required that
both the man and the woman be stoned to death.

In Romans, Paul railed against the depravity of sexual practices in
the Temples of Venus and Artemis but didn't mention them by
name. He was telling Christians not to engage in idolatry by visiting
these temples that were brothels. By that time, Paul's letters were
being read by the Roman officials before being forwarded.

The punch line that the first non-Jewish Christian. A Eunuch on a diplomatic mission for the Queen of Ethiopia. This means that not only was he transgender and a eunuch, but he was black. Stephen baptizes him.

As for the Fox News watchers, I ask what they know about transgender people. Most think like Mike Huckabee that transgender people are just jocks in dresses who want to shower with the girls. This is when a five-minute conversation about gender ambiguity can help. I'll ask them to hold up their hand and see if their ring finger is longer than their index finger. I show them my hand with the longer index finger if it's longer. Then I tell them that most girls have a longer index finger, and most men have a longer ring finger, then I ask, "What would I have to do to make my ring finger longer than my index finger?". Of course, they have no clue. "Now, if my brain was also different from yours, it's impossible to surgically change that part of my brain without killing me. Wouldn't it follow that I would have to make appropriate adjustments to match my brain?"

For complex cases, it's usually necessary to explain the difference between a guy in a dress, a drag queen, and a transgender woman.

19.4.1.5 Rewriting Biography

Another challenge for "late bloomers" is recreating their history. As a transgender girl, you were ALWAYS a girl. You might have had to keep it a secret. You might have had to try to forget that you were. You might have even forgotten for a while, but you were always a girl.

But what happens when you're talking to some people at lunch, and you start talking about yourself as a kid, when you were a boy? It can get awkward because some people might not have even known you were transgender. Others just don't want to be reminded.

It's essential to learn to tell as many of those stories as possible as a little girl. It might even be better not to mention that you were in the boy scouts or that you played baseball instead of softball. An excellent way to avoid these little slips is to encourage others to talk about themselves, which most people love to do.

20 LIFESTYLES

After transition, there are a couple of different ways to live your life. For many decades of the 20th century, most transgender people lived in stealth mode. In the 21st century, we see more transgender people living "Out and Proud."

20.1 LIVING IN STEALTH

In the late 20th century, especially the 70s, 80s, and 90s, there were few legal protections for transgender people. There were a few cities that protected the rights of gays. Women's rights included many protections for lesbians. Transgender women could still be arrested for being in public in women's clothes. Transgender girls were rounded up on suspicion of prostitution, on suspicion of avoiding outstanding warrants, or just "public indecency." Transgender women caught using a woman's bathroom could be arrested for peeping or flashing even if they kept to themselves. If they used the men's bathroom, they could be arrested for prostitution.

Even in the mid-1990s, a transgender girl living in New Jersey had to make it from a parking spot in Hoboken to the PATH train before making it to LGBT-friendly New York. There was even more risk if you came back on the PATH after 2:00 AM since Hoboken and Jersey City police were looking for "guys in dresses" who needed a restroom.

Many transgender women planned out their careers to ensure that they could succeed in the same profession as either a man or a woman. They were paralegals, lawyers, engineers, computer programmers, computer scientists, financial analysts, or even portfolio managers for mutual funds.

These people had to live in stealth mode to avoid the pitfalls and hazards. Living so that anyone could spend hours with them and only see them as women. Many were so good they stayed with their employer and simply transferred to another floor or another office.

20.1.1 BIRTH CERTIFICATE

Living in Stealth requires a complete REWRITE of history, right down to the day they were born. Transgender people who want to live in stealth have an excellent lawyer file their paperwork. They had to have the "Sex Change Surgery," but some doctors would sign off on this with as little as an orchiectomy. Often the technique was like the methods used in Witness Protection or for battered wives.

20.1.2 SCHOOL RECORDS

Changing history also required that the lawyer change all the school records. Every school transcript had to be replaced with a similar transcript with the new name and gender. Again, the lawyer was beneficial because they could pull the right strings and say the right things to minimize the resistance.

20.1.3 WORK HISTORY

Work history also had to be changed by a lawyer who knew the right way to ask and the right way to make sure it got done.

20.1.4 AWARD & DISTINCTION HISTORY

Awards and Distinctions are often harder to change. Getting a Pulitzer or Nobel Prize isn't something you can switch out. Even patents generally can't be changed once they are granted. Those need to be left out of the backstory in some cases because the trail leads back too quickly.

20.1.5 BACKSTORY

This is like what spies or protected witnesses do. They need to get and learn their own backstory so well that they won't easily blow their cover by mentioning things from their old life, especially their old name or their old gender. This is almost like being a spy.

20.1.6 PHOTOGRAPHIC HISTORY

Those who are genuinely living in stealth often eliminate their photographic history. Pictures with the parents are great, unless the boy is the only child in the picture, and you are obviously not the mother. Some people even put together doctored images of the girl in the picture. No family pictures at all can be too suspicious. Having a photo of a cousin's family or friend's family who looks like you are sometimes an option if they are old enough.

20.1.7 WHO NEEDS TO KNOW?

When living in stealth, there are still times when you must legally break cover. For example, suppose you work in the financial industry and are bonded. In that case, you need to give your true history and previous name(s). You will be fingerprinted and photographed, and the fingerprints can often be linked back to previous legal records.

You will be asked to list all your previous aliases in government positions. This is the right place to put your previous legal names and any you have used on social media. Failure to disclose this information can be a felony and causes real problems. Be especially honest if you are getting a security clearance.

20.1.8 WHO SHOULD KNOW?

Generally, HR people should know that you are transgender. Even if you can live in stealth, telling HR people can help them provide legal cover for you and help you to avoid known "problem areas". This also eliminates the risk that you could be blackmailed into doing something illegal or unethical.

Page 178 of 219

20.1.9 WHO SHOULDN'T KNOW?

Coworkers and casual friends, clients, and vendors don't need to know and probably shouldn't be told. If they do figure it out, you need to plan how to handle the situation, especially if they threaten to try and blackmail you. You want to not only be able to "call their bluff" but be able to play them out long enough to have officials witness the attempted blackmail. A bad player may be playing more than just you.

20.2 LIVING OUT AND PROUD

The other option which is much more prevalent in the 21st century is living "Out and Proud." This is much easier. The goal is to be sufficiently effective at the presentation that you don't attract attention from strangers in crowds who might turn hostile. At the same time, you don't have to try so hard to hide that you are transgender.

20.2.1 REBUILDING A NEW LIFE

A key element in being out is understanding that you may have to rebuild a new life for yourself. Create a new life that accepts the new you. When you acknowledge that your old friends, family, and coworkers may reject you, you can attract an environment supporting the new transitioning you.

20.2.2 RELOCATION

If you live in a "Bible Belt" state, in a town where guys dress up in white hoods on a Saturday night and have a little bonfire, you probably need to relocate. Most larger cities have large LGBT populations. Even if you live a little out of town, it's much easier to find accepting people in such cities and towns. There are also smaller resort towns like South Beach, Florida, Provincetown, and Fire Island, where it's straightforward to find lots of new friends and connections.

Often, the areas in the heart of LGBT communities are a bit expensive. Boys Town in Chicago, Cheeseman Park in Denver, and Castro in San Francisco will be very expensive even for a closet with a fold-down bed. Still, you can walk to the local LGBT-friendly bars and restaurants. Often, an affordable place can be found just a mile or two away.

The important thing about these communities is that the police are less likely to be hostile and phobic. The community services are better, there are support groups in the area, and medical care specializes in caring for transgender people.

Keep in mind that there is often good mass transit in these areas, and a train or bus can get you there and back, and you don't have to pay for parking.

20.2.3 EMPLOYERS

Finding a transgender-friendly employer is a great idea. A homophobic boss or company can create a hostile environment that can tear down your self-esteem as they try to force you to quit. An LGBT-friendly employer is likely to have better insurance and benefits. They may even want your help in talking with coworkers and even prospects. To such employers, being transgender isn't a liability. It's an asset.

Remember that, depending on administration policies, being a transgender woman can be worth extra EEOC points because you are transgender and a woman. If you have a wife, that makes you a lesbian, too, a triple winner.

20.2.4 GOVERNMENT ISSUES

Many companies are regulated or monitored by the government. Banks, financial institutions, insurance companies, health care facilities, and so on are all regulated by various agencies, so it's essential to be completely honest. The good news is that being out and honest can be an asset.

Being in stealth mode raises the issue of what happens if you are discovered. Being out eliminates the risks of blackmail, extortion, or strategically timed exposure.

20.2.4.1 Security Clearances

There are many different levels of security clearance, but absolute honesty is critical in all of these. You must give all kinds of history and the names of many people who know you who will be interviewed and asked if they know you are transgender.

You will also be fingerprinted and profiled, and every file in every government of every place you live may be checked. Again, trying to hide anything is a terrible idea. You may also have to take a polygraph to address many of the issues during the check. Even if you think you can beat one, it's really a bad idea to try.

20.2.4.2 Banking & Insurance

There will usually be a rather extensive background check, drug tests, fingerprints, and photographs for almost any government-regulated industry or any area where you need to be bonded or insured. Eliminating "surprises" is an excellent idea.

20.2.5 LGBTQ Support Groups

One of the great things about living out and proud and creating a life that supports that is that you have access to many more resources for the LGBTQ community. There are community centers, support groups, political support, and the opportunity to make many new connections and new opportunities.

20.2.6 CAREER CHOICES

Planning a career that provides excellent opportunities for both men and women is ideal for transgender people. Regardless of which way you are going, the transgender person can pursue careers in Information Technology, Web Development, or Cloud Technology. These are careers where they can succeed in their assigned gender, transition, and succeed in their new gender. If you have the aptitude, pursue Science, Technology, Engineering, & Mathematics (STEM) education in secondary school and college. This is also possible in healthcare professions.

20.2.7 CAREER LIMITATIONS

If you are a transgender girl, going into a very "macho" career like loading trucks or heavy lifting is a terrible idea. The HRT will reduce your upper body strength significantly. You will probably find it difficult to continue in this type of job.

If you are a transgender man, going into a female-oriented profession is also a bad idea. You might be able to work at Victoria's Secret as Victoria. Still, Victor might have more of a problem fitting in there. You might be better off at Brooks Brothers.

20.3 BLENDING IN

Another aspect of lifestyle is learning the process of "Blending in." It's OK to be Out and Proud. But going to a shopping mall in a conservative neighborhood on a Saturday afternoon wearing an evening gown or clubwear will attract a lot of the kind of attention that is not wanted.

Many who transition go through a period of "Transgender Puberty," where they dress too sexy or too glamorous for their own good. This is emotionally necessary, and the therapist can help improve the client's ability to blend.

20.3.1 PASSING

For cross-dressers and transitioning transgender girls, their initial goal is to "pass," to take the train or go shopping. They don't want people gawking, staring, and sneering, calling them "faggot" or "drag queen" in public and loudly. The one I really hated was when someone would start singing "Dude looks like a lady" or "Lola." Usually, these are alpha males, jocks, or roughnecks. They can be threatening even from across the mall and much more terrifying when they follow you into the parking lot as you approach your car.

So initially, just doing the bare minimum is a challenge. Going to a 7-11 and buying a fountain soda can be a giant leap.

20.3.2 COMPARING

A common trap during early transition is comparing yourself to the prettiest woman in the room. You'll always lose. There will always be a woman with better legs, better hair, better make-up, a prettier nose, bigger breasts. Whatever it is, you think you need to make yourself beautiful.

The danger of comparing is that one can spend vast amounts of money on plastic surgery. Facial feminization surgery, Botox, and body modifications. Then still not be the prettiest girl in the room. Comparing can make Gender Dysphoria worse.

Here's the little secret. Every woman does that at some point in their life. And even the prettiest woman in the room has her own insecurities. Eventually, a mature woman learns to accept herself. She realizes that she just needs to be the best she can be without comparing herself to others.

20.3.3 BLENDING

Next time you're in public, watch ALL the women as they walk by. Some are "dressed to impress." Others "dress for comfort." Most women are somewhere in the middle. They might be wearing cute leggings and a tunic, but they aren't torturing themselves in high-heeled boots to walk a shopping mall for 8 hours. They might be wearing trainers or boots with low heels. Comfortable yet still pretty.

The goal of a transgender woman is to BLEND with all those women. She won't be the prettiest woman in the room, but she won't be the ugliest either. She will wear clothes that are age, size, and situation appropriate. The skirt for work won't be too short, leggings or shorts for the mall, depending on temperature, and save the miniskirt for the club if you are young enough and old enough.

20.3.4 ASSIMILATING

For most transgender people, the goal is to assimilate with others of their true gender. The transgender girl wants to be "one of the girls." To be accepted, part of the group, and even popular as a girl. The transgender man wants to be "one of the guys." To be accepted and just part of a group of men with similar interests.

In their ideal world, nobody would know about their birth-assigned gender, and even if they did, they wouldn't care.

20.3.5 GETTING READ

One of the great fears from the first outing to assimilation is the fear of "getting read." Having someone see through their presentation and see their assigned gender.

The biggest fear implanted from a very young age, is some homophobic, transphobic, violent, drunk jock. Will he spot a "tell", something that betrays their true gender? Will he do a grown-up version of the bullying and beatings they got as children?

This is a genuine fear because being outed by others to someone violent by nature can turn into a dangerous situation very quickly. The number of transgender murders is relatively low because transgender women are less likely to escalate. Still, the method of death is often quite gruesome. Many transgender women do survive but are often disfigured. Transgender women have been castrated and had their shaft removed while fully conscious and awake. Some barely survive such jackknife surgeries.

Transgender men sometimes find a fair fight quickly turning into a gang rape, with disfiguring but nonfatal injuries.

This is one of the reasons that transgender people are so sensitive about being misgendered or deadnamed. Using the wrong pronoun or an old male name may seem like an innocent mistake. Still, in a bar full of half-drunk men and women, such slips can quickly spread and turn into a dangerous situation.

20.3.6 SITUATION MANAGEMENT

When a transgender person does get identified as transgender, it's crucial to have multiple strategies for handling the situation. It might be possible to diffuse the situation, or it may be necessary to resort to self-defense methods and non-lethal weapons like pepper spray.

20.3.6.1 Confrontation

The significant danger is when things shift to escalation. Transgender men often find that escalation leads to a fight with many guys who gang up. In a one-on-one fight, a transgender man has an excellent chance of winning. Still, when there are seven or eight attackers against one man, it turns out badly. Anyone with less than expert martial arts skills can quickly be overpowered and restrained. Then get raped in multiple ways. If there is any fight left after that, it can end with a trip to the hospital.

Page 185 of 219

Transgender women have even higher stakes because they lack the upper body strength and the overall physical strength to overcome even five or six men. She won't deter them long enough to run 50 or 60 feet to safety.

Using non-lethal weapons like pepper spray or keys between the fingers might buy a few seconds. Still, if they catch her, there's a good chance that those weapons will be used on her, Worse, often after they have been raped and assaulted.

What's worse, a transgender woman who does manage to disable or injure an attacker runs a very high risk of being charged with felony assault. The police won't care that it was five to one; they will arrest the transgender woman first. Even worse, the charges will be escalated. Assault becomes aggravated assault, using pepper spray or keys becomes assault with a deadly weapon, and self-defense that results in death becomes first-degree murder. This is even more true of transgender people of color.

On the flip side, the end result of the attack could be a transgender woman raped and hospitalized in an ICU. The attackers will claim "gay panic" or "transgender panic" as a defense. If they are white and rich, they will often get a plea bargain down to self-defense or simple assault, with a sentence of a few months of probation.

Put simply, escalation of any kind is almost always a losing situation for both transgender men and transgender women.

20.3.6.2 Invisibility

The most common strategy both before and after transition is invisibility. Before transition, transgender people do their best to blend with their assigned gender to survive.

During transition, they often try to limit their real-life appearances to safe spaces such as LGBT-friendly bars, businesses, and groups.

After the HRT phase of transition, they are usually very successful at blending as their true gender because it is more natural when they have about 6 months of HRT. Often, they are "read" only if someone misgenders them or deadnames them.

Part of their "invisibility" is to not draw attention directly to the slip until they are in a safe space that is more private or via private messaging.

20.3.6.3 Engagement

Ideally, the strategy with the least amount of paperwork is to try and diffuse the situation, congratulate them for noticing, laugh along with them, and answer any questions they might have. Often, they are so shocked at finding out that you really are transgender that they just become curious. Normally, the therapist has provided training and recommendations during those early real-life exercises. They learn many different strategies, and diffusing the situation becomes an excellent skill at which they are adept.

20.4 LEADERSHIP

Transgender men and women have overcome many of the challenges and obstacles involved in a successful transition. They develop many leadership qualities to succeed in business, technology, entertainment, and politics. There are many ways that Transgender people can express these leadership capabilities, both in support of their employers and clients and in support of the LGBT community.

20.4.1 BEHIND THE SCENES

Before and after transition, many transgender people find that they are most effective when working behind the scenes. They can be almost invisible and pass the correct information to the visible people. In such a way, they can influence many people and facilitate many projects and programs. This is done in such a covert way that they can simultaneously impact many different efforts.

Page 187 of 219

Often this covert influence is initially not by choice. Transgender people may approach their supervisor with a great idea and suggestions about implementing it. Their supervisor knows that if the "sissy," "faggot," or "dyke" proposes it to a group, it will be shot down regardless of its merits. The supervisor will have them write up the suggestion, add the details, and fill in more implementation details.

The supervisor will remove the cover page, put their own name, and pass it to their supervisor. This removal and replacement of attribution can often happen two or three times as it goes up the executive chain and wins sponsorship among the executive leadership.

Often, the supervisor will wait until the annual or semiannual review to use the original author's recommendations as the basis for promotions and raises, even bonuses or stock options. In many cases, management will encourage the transgender person to lead from the bottom by writing up the details as the project is implemented or encouraging them to develop new "golden eggs".

Outstanding supervisors realize that both before and after transition, he has the "goose that lays the golden eggs." One of the best examples was Lynn Conway[1]. A transgender woman who, after transition, went on to win dozens of patents for key VLSI and computer chip technologies. These patents became the cornerstone of laptops, tablets, smartphones, and smart TVs. She initiated projects worth $trillions in top-line revenue across the industry.

---

[1] Lynn Conway Transgender Engineer & Inventor

20.4.2 WRITING

Many transgender women become prolific writers. They may write from a corporate desk or freelance contributors either as a primary source of income, second income, or volunteer. There are many different channels available for those who can communicate their thoughts effectively.

20.4.2.1 Social Media

Perhaps the most common and easiest way to contribute as a writer is to contribute to social media.

Twitter tweets have very short lifecycles, and unless you have thousands of followers, most conversations disappear. On the flip side, the messages are concise, so combining a compelling text message with a meme graphic can be easily repeated. The other advantage is getting immediate feedback that can help refine and articulate arguments, positions, and ideas more effectively.

Other social media like Facebook allow longer messages and more persistence. Still, most messages need to be repeated and refined based on feedback many times to keep the conversation active.

The most effective communicators will have their messages reposted by others, extending their reach.

YouTube is a bit more of a challenge because creating videos takes more time and effort. A simple video of you talking to a camera generally doesn't do that well. Often people can be put off by your presentation. It is an excellent way to transition from writing to public speaking.

The granddaddy of social networks is Usenet, also known as google groups. The nice thing about this form of social media is writing articles that persist for decades. They can be searched by Google, and they can be used to reference other links and URLs. The challenge, of course, is that there are no pictures or figures, so mastery of the written word is essential. Written communication becomes a critical element of being a successful communicator. The other thing is that you are likely to see very long threads of disagreement. The most successful users of this media can articulately engage with critics, providing additional facts and disproving the opponents' claims. They maintain calm and reasoned arguments in the face of personal ad-homonym attacks. The goal isn't to win over the opponents calling you an idiot. It influences the observers and researchers looking for current and detailed information about the topic in question.

20.4.2.2 Blogs & Websites

The advantage of blogs is that you can contribute to someone else's blog or create your own and let others contribute to yours. You can even cross-plug across different sites on some blogs.

Setting up your own website can be more involved. Several content manager packages provide the ability to easily create new articles and pages and then provide search, browse, and browse by category capabilities that don't require massive programming or an IT degree.

Many successful authors write their more extended and complete proposals and details on their blogs. They combine it with memes or pictures to create interest, post links to the extended articles, and text to the various social media networks. When the articles are effective and popular, they will be shared, retweeted, and linked in blogs to increase viewers. Some people even pay for social media advertising that can be included in related threads, referring to the issues in question.

Several respected media outlets such as Huffington Post and Motley Fool started out as blogs and became critical resources. Sometimes, a good writer in social media or blogs will be invited to write about a specific topic. These are good ways to practice any writing you need to do professionally.

As a result, it's much easier to

20.4.2.3 Fiction Books

One of the latest breakthroughs for writers is e-publishing. Writers can write full-length novels or short stories or even anthologies or serial novels published through programs like Amazon Books, Google Books, Apple, etc. Amazon even offers the ability to convert an e-book into a print version so that an author can host book signings and other promotional events.

Some authors will write several e-books that they can publish electronically. Then they'll use that history to submit both existing books and proposed books to print publishers. They can provide publicity, promotion, and logistics necessary to move the book to various "best seller" lists or help promote the books to awards nominations. These publishers can also provide invaluable editing and content advice, helping to make the book more marketable to a broader population.

An author is much more credible if they have successfully completed three or four books. Easier to get approved than submitting an outline and the first few chapters to a publisher or literary agent. There is less "gamble" involved.

The nice thing about fiction books is that they can be "well researched." Still, there is no expectation or claim that the people are real, that events really happened, or that opinions or assertions are supported by the most current research. This can be very important if you have a friend or relative who gets irate or wants to sue you for statements made about them. Your disclaimer points out that none of the characters are real people. They could be composites of multiple people, so there are no grounds for a lawsuit, even if you use someone's name.

20.4.2.4 Nonfiction Books

Nonfiction books are much more of a challenge because you need to make some attempt to validate and authenticate at least some of your facts and assertions. This can include a substantial bibliography, footnotes, references, links, and appendices.

At the same time, one must be very careful not to violate copyrights or disclose confidential information. Information such as health or financial information that has not previously been made public. This can make citing specific case studies more difficult, especially if you must get consent from a deceased person's parents.

20.4.3 SPEAKING & APPEARANCES

Being in the front of the room as a speaker, lecturer, or teacher is challenging. Still, many transgender people take the necessary steps to do so successfully. There are even transgender politicians who have won their races. Others have spoken on behalf of candidates to help get them elected. Some transgender women have been elected as mayors and state legislators. Others have been political appointees to national offices.

We have also seen national and international celebrities like Laverne Cox, Jazz Jennings, Caitlyn Jenner, Chaz Bono, Janet Mock, Scott Turner Schofield, Zackery Drucker, Jen Richards, Rhys Ernst, Alexandra Grey, Cassandra James, Buck Angel, Rain Valdez, Zeke Smith. They have become outspoken celebrities advocating for transgender rights and being very successful performers, models, producers, and artists in their own rights.

20.4.3.1 Presentation & Appearance

When taking the front of the room, the biggest challenge is creating a presentation and appearance and communicating effectively as a post-transition transgender person. Some of the most famous transgender celebrities are beautiful women or handsome men. Only their voice even hints that they are transgender. They do NOT drag queens, guys in dresses, or even female impersonators. They are beautiful women and handsome men who are excellent performers, speakers, and presenters. They speak eloquently, tell their own story, and be very honest and open about who they are. At the same time, they can be excellent actors who can create credible characters.

20.4.3.2 Interacting with others

An important skill is interacting with others at an interpersonal level. They need to be interviewed and appear as credible resources who can present a convincing story that keeps people's attention.

20.4.3.3 Dealing with Awkward Questions

These interactions and interviews, especially with questions from an audience, can often lead to some of the "awkward" questions. They would upset transgender women being asked such questions by friends or casual acquaintances.

The difference with a large audience is that a transgender person must be careful not to be offended by these questions. Different people are prepared to answer these questions in different ways. Some refuse to talk about certain questions, but very politely. For example, Laverne Cox doesn't like to talk about the transition process and instead asks the interviewers or questioners to focus on the broader issues. Others will address these issues more directly. They explain what they have done and why. Some like Jazz Jennings have done entire documentaries on their transition process as a whole in the reality show format of the "I am Jazz" series on TLC.

20.4.3.4 Dealing with Open Hostility

Anyone who becomes a visible "knight on horseback" will always encounter "pikers" who want to knock them off the horse. This is especially true of transgender celebrities and speakers whose very existence is a political issue for religious fanatics and other homophobes and transphobes.

This is where prior social media experience can become invaluable. Whether writing their own answers or being inspired by the responses of others, these interactions become a quick resource for addressing hecklers, detractors, and other hostile actors. Some will rise to ask a "question" and spend as much time as they can get away with making a political or religious statement.

Answering these attacks calmly and effectively, using the rules of their argument against them, is an effective tool that can impress an audience and actually win hearts and minds.

20.4.4 MEDIA APPEARANCES

The nice thing about media appearances is that you have more control over the production environment, what you say, and the interactions between yourself and other people.

The other advantage is that you can start to see your own strengths and weaknesses as a speaker and performer by reviewing the video recordings. These can be short videos of just a few minutes or lectures lasting 30-40 minutes, often linked to additional related sources.

20.4.4.1 YouTube & TicToc

YouTube is a mighty vehicle for people willing to put some effort into recording, editing, and improving their presentation skills. This can be a simple speech recorded with a cell phone camera to a recording with slides and a teleprompter, to a musical production produced by media stars like Randy Rainbow.

TicToc is a more significant challenge because there are time restrictions on the length of each video. This can be an effective media because there is the discipline of delivering three to five key points in under 30 seconds. With the ability to add music, filters, special effects, and other enhancements, an experienced user can create a popular TicToc video in just a few hours.

Some tools can enhance video production, including teleprompters for either PC or cell phone, an editor for editing video and sound, and intermixing different videos and stills into the production video to reinforce the point.

20.4.4.2 Acting & Directing

There are often more people involved in more extensive and more complex productions. Doing an interview in front of the camera can often involve doing 20-30 minutes of an interview from which 2-3 minutes will be selected to be included with similar selections from other personalities.

The other opportunities in larger productions are opportunities behind the camera. As directors, editors, writers, and publicists. Some people have difficulty passing or don't feel comfortable in front of the camera. The opportunities behind the cameras can produce remarkable results.

The two transgender sisters who produced "The Matrix" series. They are perhaps the most dramatic examples of transgender women who have established themselves behind the camera. They felt free to come out as transgender after achieving phenomenal success.

Many markets such as Logo and LGBTQ advocacy groups are looking for people to manage and coordinate production and event management logistics. These are often the unknown soldiers who are the backbone of the production teams. They make the people in front of the microphones and cameras look wonderful.

20.4.4.3 Lite Productions

Often, the first step for aspiring video artists is to graduate from the simpler YouTube talking in front of a camera to more complex video production. This enables videos to be more impactful. The "talking head" video often has few followers and gets limited attention. Still, the results can be very impactful when combined with supplements such as stills, music, and videos.

Often, there are no massive legal barriers and obstacles for lite productions with limited distribution. It's important to keep track of the sources of the videos and stills being used. If something does go viral, it may be necessary to pay royalties or residuals for the source content. A music clip may be ignored for a YouTube video with only a few thousand likes. Still, the same YouTube video that gets a few million likes is likely to get more attention from those seeking royalties and those who want to further promote the video.

20.4.4.4 Green Screens

One of the simplest ways to enhance video production is using green screens. More and more during the COVID-19 shutdown, we have seen television personalities put green screens behind themselves.

The advantage of a properly lit green screen is that the green can be replaced with another background. Information from statistics to pictures of major cities to videos of critical historical events can be shown with the speaker. Often the "green screen show" can be as important as the talking head in front of the green screen.

20.4.4.5 Appearing in other's media

When appearing in the media presentations of other organizations, there are often professional make-up artists. You may be asked to bring 3-4 outfits they can choose from. There is professional lighting, and there may be 30 minutes in front of a camera with a boom microphone only inches from your head. You must focus on the interviewer, or the camera person based on the director's request.

This is often followed by 30-40 minutes with a still photographer who will take 100 or more pictures of you in numerous poses. Often, they are looking for something unusual or attention-grabbing. Usually NOT the glamour shot, the duckface, or the other classic poses we see on Snapchat or Facebook. In one case, for the New York Times, I had two full-size CRT video monitors over my shoulders on the couch while I sat between them. It looked like I was lifting them. Other times, they used the one where I looked silly or goofy. The model has no control over which images get used, so just play with it and hope their judgment is good. I have rarely been disappointed.

20.4.4.6 Control of Message?

Appearing for others has the disadvantage of not having control of the message. There may be times when you can say, "don't use that." In the long run, a good producer is going to get up to an hour of interview material in hopes of getting as little as 5-10 minutes of "Gold." That can be mixed in with other content to fill out the 40-50 minutes of programming, leaving time for ads to fill out an hour.

A good producer will listen for the speaker's commitment and try to make them look as good as possible. The interview can often go very bad in other cases, such as 60 minutes. Out of an hour of interviews, the producer picks the most negative comments, refuted by contrary evidence that is often mixed in immediately following the statement to be disproved. The result is that the subject looks like a criminal.

When offered an interview, try to know who is making the interview and their point of view. A transgender person appearing on MSNBC or Logo is likely to be treated very well. The same person on Fox or OAN will probably be painted as a villain. Make sure you do your homework before accepting such interviews.

20.4.4.7 Control of Image?

One of the most important things to be aware of when appearing publicly, whether at a Gay Pride Parade or on behalf of a political candidate. Your worst picture will be used against you. Your best picture will support you.

Showing up at an event in camp drag could show up 10 years later after you speak on behalf of transgender rights. There is no way to control which pictures are used. It's essential to try and be aware of the impact of these appearances on employers, causes, organizations, and institutions you wish to support. Perhaps the most tragic example was Caitlyn Jenner's attempt to speak out as a transgender woman and then try to speak on behalf of Donald Trump. The result was that she was no longer taken seriously as a transgender spokesperson and no longer taken seriously as a Republican.

20.4.4.8 What are your true talents?

When deciding to take on a leadership role, the most important thing is assessing your most vital talents and weak points. Avoid the camera if you sound like James Earl Jones when you speak and look like a fat drag queen on video. If you have a natural writing talent, focus on the writing and limit your public speaking events. Perhaps you can even write speeches for others who can present a better "face."

On the other hand, if you look like a fashion model and have a beautiful voice but sound like you're ranting and raving, you might want to look for someone who can write great speeches for you.

If you are good at writing short articles, then do so on social media and contribute comments to publications that are likely to publish them. You may even find yourself being asked to write as a columnist.

20.4.4.9 Maintaining Image

The most important thing to remember is that an image needs to be maintained. Becoming a national spokesperson can be a wonderful thing. Don't get arrested for getting drunk and assaulting a police officer. Don't insult a significant donor to the charity who asked you to speak. It can end your usefulness as a public influence.

Page 199 of 219

21 Summary

In summary, transgender men and women must overcome chronic traumatic stress over several years and post-traumatic stress. Being transgender is not a choice. Living authentically as their true selves is their choice. Trying to conform to their birth-assigned gender can cause acute gender dysphoria. Acute gender dysphoria is a life-threatening condition that can too often be fatal.

Transgender people are also often exceptionally gifted. They are intelligent, have extraordinary talents, and usually produce remarkable results for their employers or clients. Transition is a challenging process. Transgender people who transition, often "bloom" and are more willing to come forward and be visible as outstanding contributors to employees and their communities.

22 REFERENCES

What follows are various studies, links, and references related to the subject matter of this book.

23 RESEARCH STUDIES

24 BIBLIOGRAPHY

24.1 TRANSGENDER NON-FICTION BOOKS

24.1.1 *ALICE IN GENDERLAND: A CROSS-DRESSER COMES OF AGE*

Alice in Genderland is the first ever memoir by a crossdresser who is not content to live behind closed doors and who takes it much further than his straighter, more circumspect peers might ever care to go. Most of the time, Harvard-educated psychiatrist Richard Novic is Rick, a man at the office or a husband and father at home. But one night a week, he is Alice, a woman about town, shopping, dining, dancing, and dating a man for nearly a decade.

In contrast to the life he leads today, Rick Novic suffered since his sporty, nerdy boyhood with a secret, a desire he was in no way equipped to handle, but one that eventually burst through his denial, a few months before his wedding day. Just once, he felt, while he still could, he had to know how it felt to be a woman.

Like Alice in Wonderland, his curiosity led him to fall headlong down a rabbit hole, through desperate straits, mind-opening surprises, heart-rending changes, gritty sex, and boundless love. By the time he was back on his feet, he was a different person, living a lifestyle he hadn't known existed. Anyone who has struggled to figure out who they are and how they want to live will surely appreciate this informative and engaging life story.

24.1.2 *Christine Jorgensen: A Personal Autobiography*

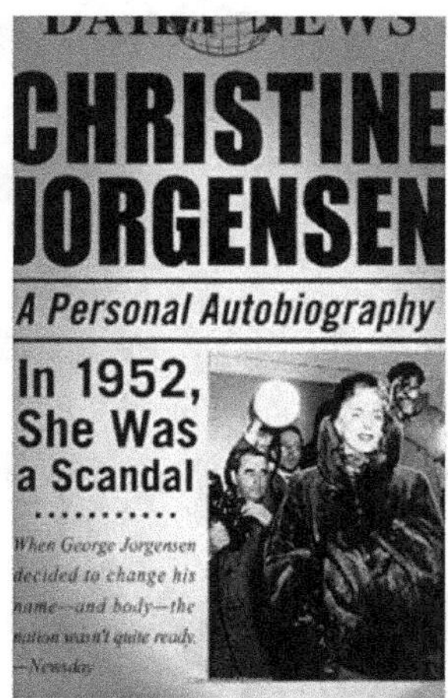

This is really the most accurate accounting of the life and transition of Christine Jorgensen written by Christine herself. The movie version was written by a former boyfriend.

In 1951 George Jorgensen, an American man of 26, left for Denmark and returned a year later as the first world-renowned transsexual, Christine Jorgensen. In her own personable style, Jorgensen offers a firsthand account of her ground-breaking life. "Nature made a mistake," she wrote, "which I have corrected."

Annie Rose changed her sex and now she explains how you can too! How To Change Your Sex: A Lighthearted Look at the Hardest Thing You'll Ever Do is an amusing and practical guide to everything you need to know for your sex change, from how to tell if you are transsexual, through venturing out in public in your new gender presentation (including which restroom to use!), to hormones and surgeries, to what to expect afterwards. Whether you are seriously considering changing your own sex, or if you have a friend or loved one who is going through the process, or even if you are just curious, you are bound to be entertained and informed by this handy little manual.

Is an extraordinary collection of real-life stories told by a wide range of sex and gender diverse people. These healing tales of struggle and transformation reveal just how creative, resourceful, and adventurous the individuals in this community can be and also helps to bridge the gap between ignorance and understanding. As each incredible story unfolds, we become part of the author's journey to self-acceptance and join the celebration of their new life. Page by page, we laugh, cry, and learn to appreciate these wonderful courageous people and the road they walked to be their true selves. *Finding the Real Me* is a landmark book that encourages us to embrace diversity, to never fear our differences, and to remain always in awe of our amazing possibilities.

Page 209 of 219

This a biographical account based upon the true-life story of Brooke

McKellogg, a young woman who was born male, yet realized at an early age she was intended to be a girl. Follow along with Bobby McKellogg, age twelve, as he finally admitted to his parents his most secret desire - to live his life as a girl. Weep with the newly renamed Brooke McKellogg as she begins her new life, still in her teen years, and learns that not everything about her new gender is as easy as she hoped it would be.

Cheer with Brooke as she undergoes her gender reassignment surgery and learns that there is indeed victory to be found when someone is willing to forge through a life fraught with setbacks and disappointments. This stirring true-to-life drama reveals the heartaches and joys of one transgender's life as she continues on as a young adult after she has undergone the gender reassignment surgery necessary in order to become the real girl she was meant to be.

Brooke McKellogg is an amazing girl the entire world will fall in love with and learn to identify with as each person reads this account of her life. Through the help of her family, friends and her own perseverance, Brooke discovers that all is worthwhile when finally able to achieve the new body, new gender, and New Life she always yearned for. What she doesn't know is what direction her love life will take as an adult woman and what form of romance she will find.

This is the first ever memoir by a cross-dresser who is not content to live behind closed doors—and who takes it much further than his straighter, more circumspect peers might ever care to go. Most of the time, Harvard-educated psychiatrist Richard Novic is Rick, a

man at the office or a husband and father at home. But one night a week, he is Alice, a woman about town, shopping, dining, dancing, and dating a man for nearly a decade.

In contrast to the life, he leads today, Rick Novic suffered since his sporty, nerdy boyhood with a secret, a desire he was in no way equipped to handle, but one that eventually burst through his denial, a few months before his wedding day. Just once, he felt, while he still could, he had to know how it felt to be a woman.

Like Alice in Wonderland, his curiosity led him to fall headlong down a rabbit hole, through desperate straits, mind-opening surprises, heart-rending changes, gritty sex, and boundless love. By the time he was back on his feet, he was a different person, living a lifestyle he hadn't known existed. Anyone who has struggled to figure out who they are and how they want to live will surely appreciate this informative and engaging life story.

What happens when you hold a secret your whole life that can never be shared? What happens when your faith abandons you to pray your problem away? What happens when you destroy a complete

generation of your family? This is the story of David, born into the Mormon faith who faces the insurmountable to become Cindi. Her life crumbles before her as she is pushed into an untenable position. Her family is destroyed as well as her career. She manages to pull herself through these agonizing events to rebuild her life and reconnect with her family.

"In this autobiography, at times whimsical and at times serious, Cindi continues to hold strong to her principles in the face of so much rejection from those around her: family, faith, friends. I believe this story can be a source of inspiration for others facing similar difficulties, by showing that acceptance from others must start with self-acceptance." ... Andrea James

2nd Edition published December 2015.The contents have been re-edited mainly to remove typographical errors. The book has been updated to include a new final chapter outlining my life in the five years following SRS and after the receipt of my new birth

certificate. This is the story of my life from earliest memories to the present day. I spent the best part of fifty years in total denial of my true gender. To the rest of the world, from my birth until I was in my mid-fifties, I was seen as male. Yet I knew from very early days, and long before I had the words to describe myself correctly, that I was in truth female. I was transsexual. I start my story on the day I told my wife why our marriage had been such a sham for the previous five years, and when I admitted to her that I was transsexual. The book progresses along two interlinked paths. One describes my early childhood and development into an adult, getting married and having children. The other path describes my journey of transition following the disclosure to my wife. It details the process up to and including my Sex Reassignment Surgery in January 2010 and the five years beyond, up to the present day. It details my receipt of a Gender Recognition Certificate and the issue of the new Birth Certificate, recording that all-important change of sex. The amendment is from the M on my original birth certificate to F on my new one, correcting the error of record at my birth and giving the book its perhaps enigmatic but wholly appropriate title.

This story is in part about the metamorphosis of a man becoming a woman, but the transformation is more than a simple change of physical appearance; It's one of spiritual and emotional change as well. Along the way, I learned things about trust, friendship, love, and the infinite ways of being human. The transition taught me

compassion for others in a way I never dreamed possible.

Sex and gender can be difficult to write about because an element of erotica, an insatiable desire that drives us as a species to reproduce, must always be addressed. For some, that lack of control can feel like a weakness that lends itself to insecurity. But I dare say, being a post-operative transsexual allows me a certain amount of freedom to discuss this subject without trepidation.

I wrote this story because I felt compelled to find peace within myself, and to that end, I've tried not to hold anything back. Transitioning from one sex to another, is no easy feat, and it's my hope that by relating my story, I can help other transgendered people prepare for their own personal journey.

I believe that everything happens for a reason. Life is not just one random event after another, but rather we are all connected. For forty-eight years, I felt I needed the world's forgiveness and felt shameful about my desire to be a member of the opposite sex. I kept those thoughts bottled up inside me for a very long time, fearful of the consequences should anyone find out the truth about me. When my father-in-law died, I felt so dishonest about my life that I couldn't take communion at his funeral. As strange as it may sound, had that not happened, I might never have found my true self.

This is the first book I've ever written, but it's a story from the heart, and I've chosen to share it because I think we all can all relate to it

Page 215 of 219

in some way. Life is a journey, and everyone's story is unique. I hope people will enjoy reading about mine.

24.1.9 *I Am Jazz*

The story of a transgender child based on the real-life experience of Jazz Jennings, who has become a spokesperson for trans kids everywhere

"This is an essential tool for parents and teachers to share with children whether those kids identify as trans or not. I wish I had had a book like this when I was a kid struggling with gender identity questions. I found it deeply moving in its simplicity and honesty."—Laverne Cox (who plays Sophia in "Orange Is the New Black")

From the time she was two years old, Jazz knew that she had a girl's brain in a boy's body. She loved pink and dressing up as a mermaid and didn't feel like herself in boys' clothing. This confused her family, until they took her to a doctor who said that Jazz was transgender and that she was born that way. Jazz's story is based on her real-life experience, and she tells it in a simple, clear way that will be appreciated by picture book readers, their parents, and teachers.

Tea and Transition

Nobody anticipated a change from heterosexual man to heterosexual woman—least of all the author herself.

This is a marvelously candid memoir of gender and acceptance; one that breaks down many complex issues, though it is her enchanting British humor that makes them such a joy to read. Inner and outer recognition is uncovered through dating debacles, painful family discussions, and trips to Victoria's Secret. Challenges of pesky pronouns, passport humiliation and underwhelming cup sizes test her spirit yet her charismatic wit never wanes. There are laugh out loud moments, heart-wrenching ones too as she tussles with the balance between he and she, and how gender is perceived—for herself and for those around her.

Back in the 80s and 90s Chase was a globe-trotting DJ who played exotic clubs in the Middle East and southern China, then an indie music radio host in Hong Kong. However, having played at rooftop parties for sheiks, been a maestro in the clubs, and a household name on the airwaves, it was only after relocating to New York that the real journey began.

Why was he feeling like a she? The feeling wouldn't go away. Then the first cross-dressing steps into Manhattan as a woman. Embarrassing wigs, stares on the subway, and heels an inch from respectability. Through painful, unexpected, and hilarious experiences, a tipping point of gender was reached. But how to tell those who knew her as a man before?

Friends were both won and lost, but the biggest announcement was over a cup of Earl Grey: the excruciating moment of disclosure with her 80-year-old mother. The devolution and rebuilding of that amazing relationship is one of the most heart-rending threads of this book.

Humor drives her forward as she explores the New York dating life as a woman. She gets thrown out of a strip club as a perceived threat to business, initiates her first bikini moment, and has a love match at the US Open Tennis Championships. Puberty happens for a renewed time in a different gender, and with that, dodgy fashion choices and overzealous make-up. She was a 16-year-old girl in her 40s.

As she considers life changing surgery, one moment of epiphany ensues, yet clarity comes with a kick. What would be next?

There are martinis on top of the world, the pyramids at dawn, and high-speed motorbike rides through Asian back streets, but Tea and Transition is far more than a globetrotting travelogue or another tale of a right-soul-in-the-wrong-body. This is a wonderfully personal journey through places beyond the physical. Of change and the human spirit, love and family values, and how one man became one woman.

The story of the first sex change, as featured in *The Danish Girl*

An inspirational and moving account of the transformation of the painter Einar Wegener, compiled from Lili's own letters and manuscripts

Lili Elbe was, in 1931, the first transsexual to receive a male-to female sex change. This remarkable book – a sensation when first published over eighty years ago – shows Lili (now the subject of a major motion picture *The Danish Girl* starring Eddie Redmayne) as a trans pioneer who took extraordinary risks to discover and liberate her true identity.

It is also a tale of marriage, of love and romance, that provides a fascinating insight to the bohemian society of the 1930s.

Lili: A Portrait of the First Sex Change is told through original documents, her personal correspondence, and with contributions from those who loved her most. Available in English as an eBook for the first time, it remains a pertinent and powerful work, acting as a monument to an iconic struggle, and a celebration of her bold and profoundly human journey.

Page 219 of 219

www.ingramcontent.com/pod-product-compliance
Lightning Source LLC
Chambersburg PA
CBHW051738250726

48659CB00001B/126